Tough Talk, Tough Texts

Tough Talk, Tough Texts

Teaching English to Change the World

CINDY O'DONNELL-ALLEN

HEINEMANN
Portsmouth, NH

Heinemann
361 Hanover Street
Portsmouth, NH 03801–3912
www.heinemann.com

Offices and agents throughout the world

Library of Congress Cataloging-in-Publication Data
O'Donnell-Allen, Cindy.
   Tough talk, tough texts : teaching English to change the world / by Cindy O'Donnell-Allen.
      p. cm.
   Includes bibliographical references.
   ISBN-13: 978-0-325-02640-4
   ISBN-10: 0-325-02640-8
   1. Language arts—Correlation with content subjects.   2. English language—study and teaching—Social aspects.   3. Critical pedagogy.   I. Title.
   LB1576.O345 2011
   371.102—dc23   2011022812

Editor: Anita Gildea
Production editor: Sonja S. Chapman
Typesetter: Cape Cod Compositors, Inc.
Cover and interior designs: Night & Day Design
Manufacturing: Steve Bernier

Printed in the United States of America on acid-free paper

15   14   13   12   11   VP   1   2   3   4   5

For Beth, Cam, and Rebecca,

world's greatest thinking partners

Contents

In Cindy O'Donnell-Allen's worldview, teachers and students coexist in mutual respect and happiness.

Yes, *happiness*.

Why are we so ready to ban happiness from learning? Learning should infuse the learner with joy. *Tough Talk, Tough Texts* shows us how that can be achieved by introducing students to challenging books and allowing them to engage in meaningful discussions.

What teacher anywhere does not yearn to see his students truly engaged in learning? What teacher does not want students to think of learning as an eagerly pursued lifestyle rather than an oppressive, claustrophobic hour in a dreary room studying antiseptic formulas that have nothing to do with life? What teacher's heart does not cry out to honor her valid instincts, her authentic sense of what true education is and can be—nothing short of changing the world through the students she interacts with every day?

Tough Talk, Tough Texts is a catalyst for awakening teachers' hearts and minds and reminding all of us who work with young people about the danger of throwing away the lifeblood of our students' interior worlds and our own dreams of changing the world for the better. Rather than limiting students with cumbersome carbon-copy texts linked to standardized tests, *Tough Talk, Tough Texts* insists that we offer students books that are not simply large, bulky Hallmark cards but that instead challenge them to consider difficult issues, push them to think deeply and grow.

Foreword

Jimmy Santiago Baca

Rather than train the mind to tolerate social poisons such as racism, inequality, sexism, and purposeless violence, why not help students learn to understand them and respond by means of civil, intelligent discourse? It's no use pretending these poisons don't exist—they are everywhere—and students must be afforded some way of coping. We must not only teach tolerance for opposing points of view but also help students develop the moral and intellectual fortitude to face down and transcend inequity.

O'Donnell-Allen proposes a curriculum that allows students to taste the harsh but nutritious elixir of experience thoroughly worked over by lived disappointments, dreamy aspirations, and creativity taken to task by real-world limitations. She advocates for books and classroom discussions that allow students to make their own singular and unique choices, choices that may fail them yet always invigorate their sense of being alive. To teach students to become critical thinkers, we need to help them face the moment's drama rather than escape it. We need strong minds and young hearts capable of forgoing their safety nets, leaving their comfort zones, so that we can move forward as a society. We need to heal the fractures, unite the splinter groups, and penetrate the darkness of our own fears with the illuminating beams of solutions. We lose a wealth of teachable moments when the experiences we learn from most are the ones ignored in the classroom.

True teaching, authentic learning, is stronger and carries more of a wallop, impacts students in deeper and more lasting ways, than all the pop-culture gadgetry that surrounds students today. Books that contain words thoughtfully spoken, ideas intelligently worked out, no matter how harrowing and filled with misery and hardship, teach so much more than the latest mobile phone apps, YouTube titillations, and show-off name-brand clothing. Life gift-wrapped in technology corrupts young minds, diverts them from learning how to live a life fulfilled by meaning, purpose, direction, and compassion.

Tough Talk, Tough Texts gives us the tools to touch our students' hearts, reform our educational models, and turn the classroom into a world of flourishing young minds that will go on to shape society in their image. There can be no more beneficial and rewarding realization than to see oneself included in the continuing fabric of humanity. And the wonderful thing is, the student can journey as far he wishes, as far as her heart and mind desire to go.

If education does anything, it must renew one's sense of being alive. Living is learning, and we must guide our young people to a place within themselves where they again love to learn, both in a social context and in a private, meditative context. *Tough Talk, Tough Texts* leads us up that steep mountain path and enables us to arrive intact and filled with vision.

Like Steven Church, author of *The Guinness Book of Me*, I was fascinated by *The Guinness Book of World Records* when I was a kid. So much so that I wanted to write my own, but how to compete with the world's longest mustache, fastest turkey plucker, or farthest eyeball popper? What fame could a ten-year-old really claim?

Most Easy-Bake Oven cakes made in one day.

Greatest number of pennies saved in a Cool Whip container.

Longest Barry Manilow marathon ever performed on an upright piano.

As impressive as those records might have been in 1975, I knew I'd have to wait a few decades to fill an entire book. Now, I get my chance because I currently hold a world record of my own: Writer, Most Grateful. So by the power vested in me, I award the following world records to those who've played a part in the creation of this book:

Students, Savviest. Elizabeth Lewis, Cameron Shinn, and Rebecca Garrett have allowed me to eavesdrop on their students' good thinking for the past several years. Their prowess in engaging in civil discourse inspired this book. My own student, Stephanie Griffin, graciously agreed to take my photograph for the back of the book.

Teacher-Researchers, Most Committed. Cam, Beth, and Rebecca immerse themselves in the craft of teaching and fearlessly reflect on and refine their work. They've allowed me to watch and work alongside them and have given up many a planning period so that we could figure out what civil discourse really is and how to help students sustain it on a daily basis. They are the English teachers I want to be when I grow up.

Acknowledgments

Professional Home, Sturdiest. Teaching is the hardest job I've ever loved. My involvement in the National Writing Project has helped me stick with it since 1987. I was taught by a writing project teacher, joined up early in my own career, and have been lucky enough to direct a site for the past several years. Thanks are especially due to Pam Brown, Tanya Baker, and the teachers in the Colorado State University Writing Project. They remind me often that inquiry, critique, and celebration are equally essential to doing hard work well.

Colleagues, Most Collegial. Louann Reid and Pam Coke asked me how this project was going just often enough to convince me that others needed to hear about it. They bought lattes. They scheduled colloquia with colleagues and preservice teachers that helped me to see how these ideas played before a live audience and to understand how to revise them accordingly. Others should be so lucky to work with a duo as dynamic and generous as this one.

Editorial Staff, Best Ever. My editor, Jim Strickland, is a writer's best friend—an expert in cajoling, encouragement, and sentence repair. When my pen hovers over a student paper, I've learned to ask myself what Jim would say to help the writing and the writer grow. He's made this a better book and me a better writer. I treasure his wit, wisdom, and winning smile. Without Sonja Chapman, Eric Chalek, Anita Gildea, Lisa Luedeke, Maura Sullivan, and all the folks at Heinemann, you wouldn't be holding this book in your hands.

Family, Most Faithful. My parents, Jim and Betty O'Donnell, fed my insatiable appetite for reading and bought me a talking Dr. Doolittle doll when I was three. I've been interested in books and discourse ever since. My mother-in-law, Cynthia Courtney, continues to display my first book on its own little stand in her living room. Now, at long last, she has a matched set. My children, Lexie, Lynley, and Austen, have long demonstrated extraordinary forbearance with their perpetually distracted mother. They know that "let me just finish this section" really means we're having pizza for dinner, and they have pretended to be okay with that. My husband, Will Allen, has known me since I was eight and chose to marry me anyway. I am ever so grateful because he is still my very best friend. Thanks to all of them, my heart and my life are blessedly full.

The last time someone asked you what you did for a living, I'm guessing you answered, "I teach English" or "I teach middle school [or high school] students." I'd be surprised if your answer was "I change the world." Because you picked up this book, however, I bet that's what you believe to be true all the way down to your bones.

I began writing this book in an attempt to better understand the classrooms I have visited where I saw English teachers and their students daily changing the world by pulling off extraordinary conversations about difficult literature. Whether the classroom was rural or suburban, middle school or high school, advanced or alternative, racially and economically diverse or homogeneous, I have heard students discussing some of the most difficult issues of our times purposefully, intensely, and with maturity far beyond their years.

Listening to hundreds of spirited conversations, I've wondered, *Exactly how are these kids able to tackle a problem that many adults in our culture apparently cannot; that is, how can they engage in tough talk about race, class, religion, and war, especially among those with whom they may disagree?* Indeed, I imagine that an outsider eavesdropping in these classrooms would probably do a double take. While rousing the rabble about a controversial topic requires little effort or finesse, exploring it thoughtfully and respectfully is a different matter altogether.

Introduction

Change a Classroom,
Change the World

A Culture of Controversy

In our time, controversy abounds and, more often than not, divides. This cultural moment is dominated by trash-talking celebrities and professional athletes, politically partisan sound bites, spin-doctored news, and reality TV shows that make it appear "difficult to deal, except in a ridiculing way, with issues of any complexity" (Gardner 1996, 60). In fact, while I was writing this book, rapper Kanye West leapt on stage during the Vocal Music Awards, grabbed the microphone from Taylor Swift while she was accepting an award, and declared that it should have gone to Beyoncé Knowles instead; Senator Joe Wilson shouted "You lie!" on the House floor during President Obama's speech on health care to a joint session of Congress; and tennis star Serena Williams verbally attacked a line judge during the U.S. Open.

All this in the space of one week.

When pressed, all three offered excuses rather than true apologies: Kanye West said that his actions were the result of not taking time off after his mother's death two years before. Joe Wilson apologized to the president through the White House Chief of Staff; on his website, however, Wilson accused those who opposed his actions of "using my vocal opposition as an excuse to muzzle the American people," and then asked, "Will you please make a donation to help me fight back against these unwavering attacks?" Serena Williams said that she did not remember her outburst, adding "I am not a robot. I have a heart and I bleed."

Our world may not be more fraught with personal, social, and political conflict than at any other time in history. But the erosion of general civility, the trend toward polarization, and the unquestioned acceptance of popular media and their views make these conflicts more emotionally charged and less easily negotiated than ever before. Still, I believe that many people in our culture, including many young people, are up to the task of addressing this problem, of figuring out how to bore through the complexity of difficult issues without clamming up or coming to blows. In terms of the first option, we need look no further than a storybook example to see how things turned out for the unclothed emperor. Ignoring or suppressing the obvious inevitably leads to someone's demise. The second option is even less productive; we can look to recent history to see how forgone diplomacy can result in armed conflict.

Just where can today's young people learn to make up their own minds about issues that matter deeply in our culture but are likely to engender conflict when they arise? As Robert Probst has pointed out, "There aren't many models of civil discourse for our students to learn from" (2007, 45). When young people look to adults, they are more likely to see examples of highly agenda-driven communication. Without intervention, the next generation may become chair-flinging, shout-'em-down bullies who see verbal, emotional, and physical violence as a viable way to resolve conflict once and for all.

Creating a Culture of Civility

This book, however, is based on the hopeful premise that English teachers can help students learn to exercise literacy to promote civility and social justice. By wrestling with tough texts on culturally sensitive issues, your students can learn to pose and grapple with questions like those posed by students in the classrooms I describe in the pages to come:

"What does it mean to make a difference in the world?"

"Is peace possible?"

"If you can't change big things in our world, do small changes matter?"

With careful preparation students can learn to pose and discuss such questions even when you are not in charge of the conversation. And in the service of learning to listen and respond with empathy to one another, they can implement strategies that will allow them to become more critical and strategic readers, writers, and thinkers, both in and outside your classroom.

This idea emerged over the course of several years as I worked with English teacher Rebecca Garrett and her tenth graders to convene book clubs in their pre–advanced placement classroom. Originally, Rebecca decided to try book clubs because both of us believe they provide authentic contexts for reading.

Book clubs allow students to choose the books they read and how they interpret them. We like book clubs for the curricular flexibility they provide for teaching sound response strategies, and we know that students, like readers outside school, typically enjoy the social aspects of book clubs. Most of all, though, we appreciate book clubs' potential for helping students become more independent and able readers of complex literature.

Each semester, though, when we determined which books to use, we focused increasingly on those with culturally sensitive topics because these books seemed to prompt the deeply engaged conversations we were hoping for; furthermore, these books really seemed to *matter* to the kids beyond the school context. During discussions of these books, students would lean forward as they spoke and cock their ears toward the speaker in order to hear better. Rebecca and I began to wonder just what was going on.

We were equally curious about how we could help students address the sticky subjects that we felt sure they were purposefully ignoring. At the beginning of Aidan Chambers's *Postcards from No Man's Land*, for instance, the main character, Jacob, converses with a beautiful young woman in an outdoor eatery in Amsterdam. By the end of their conversation, the woman lets Jacob know in no uncertain terms that "she" is actually a "he." Even though this scene is crucial to the plot and character development of the novel, students wouldn't touch it.

Over several semesters, Rebecca and I talked about the discussions that were (and weren't) occurring in book clubs. What surprised us was that the same texts could provoke these seemingly opposite reactions. This observation suggested that it wasn't just the students, and it wasn't just the books, but something about the combination of the two. The book clubs we deemed most successful were those in which students were able to confront matters of cultural significance as they came up in texts rather than simply glossing over or giggling about them— the clubs in which students didn't back away from the hard questions the books raised but wrote and spoke about them more earnestly than we typically saw students approaching subjects in school. Book club discussions often continued beyond the walls of Rebecca's classroom and seemed to matter to the kids beyond good grades and teacher approval.

A conversation I had with one of the book clubs in Rebecca's class gave me some insight into why this was the case. On this particular day, I was circulating among the book clubs as they created their final projects, a visual interpretation assignment called the Map Project (see Chapter 6 for the full assignment).

The book club whose members created the map in Figure I.1 had read Meg Cabot's *How I Live Now*, a novel written from the perspective of sixteen-year-old Daisy, who has just survived a third world war. While students sketched on a large sheet of butcher paper, they explained to me the significance of several of the symbols they had drawn. Then Amber[1] said, "What I don't get is how we have to learn a bunch of facts about World War II and the Vietnam War in school, but we never get to talk about the war we're in right now. Why is that?"

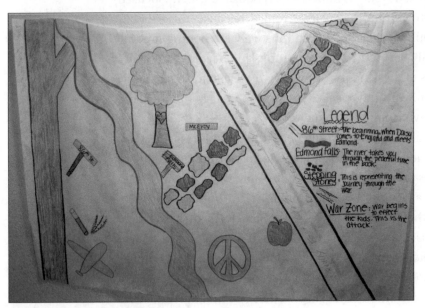

Figure I.1 - *How I Live Now* map

Curious about their theories, I kicked the question back to the group. The students reasoned aloud that in these litigious times, teachers and administrators are generally worried about the consequences of raising controversial topics in class. The group's consensus about whether teachers should be able to express their viewpoints on such topics was unanimous: they thought teachers should say what they think as long as they don't attempt to impose their viewpoints on students. The group was adamant that teachers should not take the safe route by ignoring difficult issues altogether; as Amir reasoned, "We are at the age when we should be allowed to start making up our own mind."

If I'd ever doubted its significance before, these students reminded me that teaching English is about far more than meeting standards. Weighed down by mandate upon mandate and test upon test, it can be hard to remember why we got into this teaching business in the first place. But our English classrooms in

[1]All student names are pseudonyms.

particular are ideal laboratories in which students can experiment with making up their own minds, as Amir put it, about the issues that all of us must eventually confront if we are to have any hope of building a more socially just world.

Teaching English Can Change the World

This is a bold claim. But I believe it can. Think about the topics that generally come up when people are polled about the issues that concern them most with regard to our nation. Typical items on the list are war and other political conflicts; issues related to class, race, and sexual identity; and areas of social concern, such as religious values, gender equity, the right to life and the right to choose, and so forth. Now ask yourself, what skills would be necessary to address *productively* the complex challenges and issues that emerge when a wide range of people are unlikely to see eye to eye?

How might people express their viewpoints when walking on potentially dangerous ground? Verbally? Visually? In writing? Perhaps through some combination of the three? Would they need to be able to read and interpret complex texts? Would they have to listen well in order to understand varying perspectives on the issues? Would they be likely to use technology to find out more information and communicate their viewpoints about the topic at hand? Questions like these make it clear that whatever it might take to change the world, the literacy skills students develop and hone in our English classrooms will be at the heart of it. In this book, I've included some concrete strategies that will help students acquire them.

How to Use This Book

I've organized this book to reflect the sequence of support that students need as they engage in tough talk about tough texts. The chapters that follow often feature book clubs as the centerpiece of this approach. I believe that book clubs[2] are one of the most "consistently reliable" practices around for "approximating

---

[2]A brief but important clarification of the term: I define *book clubs* as "small groups of readers that meet on a regular basis to systematically discuss books (and other texts) of the members' choice" (O'Donnell-Allen 2006, 1). Even though the terms are often used interchangeably, book clubs differ from literature circles, small-group discussions, and reading groups in important ways. Rather than relying on "role sheets" (Daniels 2002) or study questions created by a teacher, book clubs use open-ended response tools to foster conversations that tend to be less formatted and more student-directed than those occurring in the other contexts just mentioned.

out-of-school contexts where readers explore texts they've chosen in the challenging but supportive company of others" (O'Donnell-Allen 2006, 51). However, as you'll soon see, the method I describe isn't limited solely to book clubs but includes a combination of whole-class and small-group discussion of texts with a good bit of reflection on both. That's because helping students engage in tough talk with tough texts takes some practice going in. I recommend that you start students off with whole-class discussion of some "starter texts" that everyone reads in common.

If you aren't ready to incorporate book clubs into your curriculum just yet, all of the strategies in this book are certainly adaptable to whole-class study of the same text, play, or other book-length work. If you take this tack, simply substitute "small-group discussion of literature" any time you see "book clubs."

Whatever approach you take to using these strategies, small-group discussion is essential if students are to meet the objective that I argue for in this book. If we hope to help students transfer these strategies to settings outside school, we need to allow them some practice engaging in tough talk independently of us. Of course, we'll be nearby to provide support when needed. But if the classroom discussion is always teacher-directed, the likelihood that students will be able to tackle tough topics when we aren't there to supervise is slim indeed (Marshall, Smagorinsky, and Smith 1994).

In the first chapter, I focus on the fundamentals, fleshing out the concepts of *tough talk* and *tough texts* and describing the underlying principles for teaching both. In Chapter 2, I offer a rationale for why the entire enterprise of teaching students to talk about tough texts is worthwhile, and in Chapter 3, I address the practical matter of selecting frequently challenged books and generating rationales to teach them.

Chapter 4 centers on the mind-set and skill set students will need to engage in tough talk about tough texts. I describe different sequences and strategies you can use to scaffold students' learning as they move through what I call a *civil discourse sequence* (CDS), that is, from whole-class to small-group discussions of texts focused on progressively more difficult issues.

Chapter 5 explains how to help students sustain independent discussions of tough texts and provides guidelines for grouping students, setting norms, and using the response tools in small groups. I describe student and teacher tools for documenting discussions and include additional techniques you can use to support student interaction like drop-in visits, individual conferences, and WebQuests.

Chapter 6 tackles the question *how do I know my kids are getting it?* with "it" referring to both the development of civil discourse skills and the content of the tough text itself. The chapter provides multiple resources for assessing students' work at the conclusion of a CDS.

In the final chapter, I revisit the book's original premise and examine the implications of viewing literacy teaching and learning as advocacy for social change.

The figures you'll see throughout the chapters feature important concepts, procedures, and student samples, and you can find reproducible handouts, assignment sheets, and scoring guides on this website: www.heinemann.com/toughtalk. (If you're reading this book with colleagues, you may also be interested in the "Questions for Group Study" at the back.)

Making Social "Ch-Ch-Changes": Moving from Premise to Practice

Is it possible to teach English in a way that changes the world? Believe it or not, I think David Bowie can lend some insight here. In his song "Changes," Bowie chides his presumably adult audience for their cynicism and suggests that young people ought not be excluded from the negotiations that might bring about change in the world. Although our instinct as teachers may be to spin our classrooms into cocoons with gauzy walls that buffer students from tough realities, shouldn't they have a say right here, right now, about the future of our country and our world?

After spending the past few years watching students wrestle with issues and questions that adults alternately come to blows about or politely avoid, I'm convinced the answer is a resounding *yes*. In fact, my friend and colleague Louann Reid joked that the subtitle for this book ought to be *Yes, Kids Really Can Do This!* (I thought it would be a good idea to add . . . *Even If Adults Can't.*) Although it might seem unlikely at first glance, it's true that with mindful support, students can learn to acknowledge and negotiate existing tensions—within texts, classrooms, and the real world. Literature grants readers vicarious access to a vast range of worlds beyond our own; our English classrooms can provide venues for helping students engage in civil discourse on the pressing issues of our time.

I am convinced that this skill is too essential to our world's well-being to leave to chance. Facility with civil discourse persuades allies and enemies alike to come to the table and stay there. And it enables the work they will do after they leave. That's why this book is about more than selecting multicultural literature, teaching literacy strategies that are theoretically sound, or subscribing to the principles of social justice, although it acknowledges the importance of all of these things. At its heart, *Tough Talk, Tough Texts* is about teaching English to change the world both in the future and *now*. In the end, doing so is not necessarily about changing kids' minds but about furnishing them with the opportunities and skills they need to generate and articulate their own thoughts about the issues that matter deeply to all of us.

Chapter 1

I'm a stickler for definitions, especially in education. We often assume a common reference point when using terms like *achievement, authentic learning,* and *educational reform.* But I wonder how often we fall into the same trap as the legendary blind men attempting to describe an elephant; even though we assume a shared reality, we're describing it only in terms of our own experience, which may bear little if any resemblance to someone else's experience. To avoid the same mistake, I devote this chapter to defining tough talk and tough texts. I want to make sure that we are indeed on common ground.

I have an ulterior motive as well, which is to quiet any suspicion remaining in the back of your mind that teaching tough talk about tough texts is a grand idea in theory but would never work in your classroom with your kids. My definition of both terms came about in an effort to describe what was happening when kids talked in productive—and sometimes not so productive—ways about difficult texts. In other words, the successful classroom practice I witnessed necessitated a theory that made sense of it, not the other way around. Further, the three terrific

Describing the Elephant
Conversations That Matter and the Books That Make Them Possible

teacher researchers who field-tested the strategies I present in this book work in vastly different classrooms and adapted their approaches according to their students' needs.

Cameron (Cam) Shinn welcomed me into his sixth-grade rural classroom, Rebecca Garrett into her tenth-grade pre-AP English classroom, and Beth Lewis into her multiage English and humanities classes at an alternative high school. Over a period of three years, Cam, Rebecca, and Beth allowed me to work closely with their students as they used the strategies and resources featured in this book; I even team-taught with them on occasion. All of us recorded field notes of our observations of students' interactions and spent many hours poring over student work together and preparing for local and national presentations about what we were finding. I draw on this data throughout the book to demonstrate how students regularly exceeded our expectations and complicated our understanding as well. I've tried to capture what Mike Rose (2009) calls "the public good through the details of classroom life . . . [in order to] convey in a specific and physical way, the intellectual work being done day to day . . . the feel and clatter of teaching and learning" (153–54) as it occurred in these classrooms.

Reading about what went on in Beth's, Cam's, and Rebecca's classrooms will allow you to see that tough talk about tough texts is possible in a range of contexts and should also help you gauge what adjustments you'll need to make to strategies and procedures before using them with your students. Even though all three of them teach in the same large district and their schools lie within a ten-mile radius of one another, the demographics, school philosophies, and community sensibilities are profoundly different.

Cam's Classroom: A Rural School

Cam teaches in Belton Plains,[1] a rural community, population 2,700. Many of his students' parents tell Cameron that they prefer to live in the community because it provides a "family values" atmosphere within ten miles of a larger city. Those ten miles might as well be a hundred, however, because like many farming and ranching communities, Belton Plains has a sleepy, middle-of-nowhere feel. In the early 1900s, sugar beets were the cash crop that persuaded the Colorado and Southern Railroad to connect Belton Plains to the rest of the world via rail. Once

[1]All place names are pseudonyms.

billed as the "Lamb Capital of the World," the town still refers to itself as an "agri-cultural paradise." The twenty-five-miles-per-hour speed limit is strictly enforced.

As I write this, the larger district of which Belton Plains is a part just completed a grade reconfiguration that shifted sixth graders from elementary to middle schools. Even though sixth graders were already considered middle schoolers in the vast majority of the state, at the time we conducted our research, Cam's students were housed in Belton Plains Elementary, a K–6 school with a population of around 700 students. While 77 percent of the students are white, the 20 percent Latino popula-tion is growing rapidly. The remaining 3 percent of students are African American, Asian American, or Native American. Thirty-five percent of the students receive free or reduced-price lunches.

Flanked by farmland on two sides and small-frame houses and the junior high football field on the others, Belton Plains Elementary is a modern version of a coun-try schoolhouse. The sand-colored building has a bright-blue peaked roof with a large clock steeple above the entrance and is nestled among a few large cotton-woods and blue spruce trees. Two classroom wings branch off from the main office. To ease the directionally challenged, each hallway is marked with the character traits the school emphasizes. To get to Cam's classroom, you take a right at Respect Avenue and travel east down Responsibility Boulevard.

To distinguish the character of Belton Plains Elementary from other schools in the district, Cam's colleagues, many of whom live in Belton Plains themselves, have collected a set of "Beltonisms," all in good fun. We added an honest-to-goodness new one during the writing of this book: *When a student misses book club to ride barrels in a rodeo competition, you know you're in Belton Plains.*

Rebecca's Classroom: An Affluent High School

Rebecca teaches in an affluent high school of around 1,200 students, grades 10–12, located in the larger city that lies about ten miles south of Cam's school. This city of about 142,000 is home to one of the state's largest universities. Its picturesque his-toric district, bioscience and tech industry, and easy access to outdoor sports of all kinds repeatedly earn it a top-ten spot on *Money Magazine*'s Best Places to Live list.

Established in 1890, Legacy High School is the district's first high school and was originally located in the center of the city just across from the university. Because of increasing enrollment, Legacy relocated in 1995 to a new building nationally known for its stunning architectural design. A white sail-shaped tower stands over 170 feet tall in front of the building, a feature inspired by lyrics from the school song. Natural light pours in through floor-to-ceiling windows that line a hallway with a curved cathedral ceiling. The hallway is a quarter-mile spine that runs the length of the building, connecting its separate wings.

Despite its modern appearance, Legacy's pride in its heritage is evident from the moment you enter the building. Trophy cases lying just to the left of the entrance house a purple-and-gold letterman's sweater, a wool pennant and megaphone, and tarnished victory cups. Solemn girls in snow-white dresses and boys with oiled hair and wire-rimmed glasses peer out from sepia-toned class photographs. According to its website, the school features strong traditional curriculum and values and still encourages students to wear their school colors "often" and "with pride." Every Friday afternoon, an a capella choir sings the alma mater on the staircase of the main wing.

Rebecca is proud to be a Legacy graduate and leads the school spirit club. Close to fifty extracurricular opportunities are listed on the school website, including a student news program produced in the school's video studio, science and math Olympiads, rock climbing and fishing clubs, and Amnesty International. In recognition of their extracurricular activities, Legacy has received the state's prestigious Wells Fargo Cup. The school also offers an impressive slate of advanced-placement and honors classes and features programs unique from the other four high schools in the district, including courses in computer chip design, the hospitality industry, and fashion design.

The school population is 77 percent white and 16 percent Hispanic, with the remaining 7 percent African American, Asian American, or Native American combined. The school has no Title 1 program. In fact, with just over 2 percent of the students receiving free or reduced-price lunches, Legacy is easily the most affluent of the district's five high schools.

Beth's Classroom: An Alternative High School

By contrast, Beth teaches at Century High School, an alternative school that is the last-chance Texaco for most of its 135 students. A handful of students elect to attend the school by their own volition, but most have been dismissed from mainstream schools for various offenses, including fighting, drugs, arrests, poor grades, and high absenteeism.

Located in the older part of the same city as Legacy High, Century High is housed in a former elementary school built in 1903. Even though the old two-story building has been refurbished and sports a new addition that carefully matches its architectural style and the original clay brick, entering the school feels like going back in time. Just past the front doors, the creaky floor gives a little underfoot, belying the presence of wood beneath the speckled gray industrial carpet. An aquarium glows blue next to a standard waiting-room chair to the left of the dimly lit entrance. While administrative offices and rooms in the new wing look as modern as any of those found in newer schools in the district, the rest of the school is vintage.

To get to Beth's room, you walk down the hallway past a wide, banistered staircase flanked by large plants that soak up the sun from the high window near the base of the stairs. Job advertisements are written on chalkboards that line the hallway since many of the students support themselves financially. Ceilings are at least twenty feet high here, so the building feels spacious and cool in warm weather, yawning and drafty in cold.

Right outside Beth's room is a large open area that functions as a commons with long tables, chairs, and a couple of donated couches. On the white walls, recent student projects hang next to quilts with blocks handmade by former graduating classes. Sometimes while passing from class to class, students will pause just long enough to play a quick tune on the old upright piano in the hallway or lean over the white porcelain water fountains still sized for small children. Teachers store their bikes in an old cloakroom nearby.

Beth keeps community supplies on hand in her classroom—a silver coffee can full of scissors, free pencils, and spiral notebooks—and routinely provides peanut butter sandwiches for students to eat on field trips, since 34 percent of Century students receive free or reduced-price lunches and a good number of those are "couch surfers," students' hip euphemism for "homeless." Seventy-three percent of the students are white, 23 percent are Latino, and the remaining 4 percent are Native American or African American. A few years ago, the school secured funds to put in a shower and buy a washer, dryer, detergent, and bath soap so that students could bathe and launder their clothes at school. A big event every year is the traditional Thanksgiving dinner the staff prepares for the students, many of whom would otherwise go without. Teachers stress individual accountability at Century High, but they help students achieve it in a community that cares.

At first glance it might seem unlikely that a similar instructional approach would work in classrooms as diverse as Belton Plains Elementary, Legacy High School, and Century High School, but Beth, Cam, and Rebecca used the same basic set of strategies, assignments, and resources to complete the civil discourse sequence that you'll read about in subsequent chapters. Of course, experienced teachers know that whether we're talking school to school, class to class within the same school, period to period, or year to year, what counts as a "best practice" in one context might need to be tweaked or overhauled in another. The same is true for the methods featured in this book. What's essential to remember is that *you* know your students, your school, and the community's sensibilities better than anyone else. When you see the adaptations we made in Beth's, Cam's, and Rebecca's classrooms, I hope you'll get the message: don't be afraid to substitute texts and adapt strategies for *your* classroom as you see fit.

What Is Tough Talk?

Tough talk refers to the specialized communication students use to address the controversial topics that arise in tough texts, texts that raise difficult issues and treat them in complex ways. Conversations that matter—the kind authors have with their readers, readers have with other readers, and all of us as citizens have with one another—often require tough talk or *civil discourse*, two terms I'll now use interchangeably.

Even though the latter term is widely used outside the classroom, I was surprised to learn that it is seldom if ever defined, at least as far as I, numerous university librarians, multiple search engines, and the writers of the *Oxford English Dictionary* can tell. Although the lack (and by *lack* I mean the complete absence) of a definition was initially fascinating to me, it soon became quite troubling. Perhaps the missing definition suggested something larger about us as a culture. Even though we Americans often take pride in our messy democracy, I began to wonder if our inability to sort through all the messes had something to do with our neglect in defining this term.

My search for a definition of civil discourse began innocently enough, but it soon became a quest, not just for me but for Rebecca and her students as well. It lent importance to our work because it showed us how important definitions really are in the classroom and the culture at large. I think you'll find our journey instructive.

Early on in our work together, Rebecca and I assumed we shared definitions of civil discourse without discussing the term in much detail. That changed when we realized that we needed to introduce the term to her tenth graders, who would probably find it unfamiliar. To that end, we wanted to feature an "official" definition at the top of a handout that would guide students' first civil discourse book club activity. I agreed to look for the best definition for our purposes—

we assumed there would be several—and headed straight to www.merriam -webster.com, my favorite online dictionary.

Surprisingly, I had no luck there. Still, I figured the task would be straightforward enough that it would take a matter of minutes, especially when my Google search turned up 295,000 hits in thirteen hundredths of a second. Although I didn't wade through every single hit, two hits near the top of the list were a Wikipedia entry and another more dubious site that offered a definition but also featured links to sites like "mathsux.com." Even civildiscourse.com, which describes itself as "an open, thought-provoking forum on issues of the day," offered guidelines for engaging in civil discourse without ever defining it. I was puzzled, but not disheartened, a little excited even, by the prospect of digging through the more exhaustive dictionaries at the university library.

In the meantime, the term serendipitously began popping up in the local and national news. The hubbub was in response to the infamous tasering incident that occurred at the University of Florida in the fall of 2007. There, a twenty-one-year-old University of Florida student named Andrew Meyer was tasered, restrained, and arrested after his outburst at a university forum where Senator John Kerry was speaking. Video of the event immediately hit YouTube and CNN. At the same time that University of Florida students were organizing protest rallies and invoking the First Amendment over Meyer's treatment, speculation arose about whether the event was staged or authentic since the student was well known for his outspoken blog and prior outlandish stunts.

Meanwhile, *The Rocky Mountain Collegian*, the student newspaper at Colorado State University, where I teach, reacted with this four-word editorial: "Taser this . . . [expletive] Bush," an apparent attempt to draw a parallel between the authorities' attempts to silence Andrew Meyer and the Bush administration's alleged attempts to silence political opposition at Bush's town hall meetings. A flurry of reactions followed on *The Collegian* website, setting an all-time record for response to the paper's editorials, and a range of letters, from outraged to supportive of the editorial staff, ran in *The Collegian* and other newspapers statewide. Local sponsors began withdrawing financial support from the university paper, whose managing editor, J. David McSwane, quickly issued a response standing by the paper's decision to run the editorial.

Ultimately, the University of Florida and Colorado State University imposed consequences on Meyer and McSwane, but what interested me most was the reaction of both university presidents, who publicly reiterated their institutions' commitment to civil discourse, again without ever defining the term. While I am encouraged that universities and other American institutions claim to be committed to the concept of civil discourse, what exactly are Americans sharing a commitment to if the term is never defined? The void suggests that we apparently know civil discourse when we see it or, in the above cases, when we don't.

While pondering these questions would have been terrifically interesting for Rebecca and me over a series of languid summer days, we had a handout breathing down our necks. In the end, we decided to delay our library search for an official definition and to do what inquiry-oriented teachers typically do in the face of unanswerable questions: we passed the task along to the kids by asking them to generate a working definition of the term based on some scenarios we'd seen play out in book clubs where students used discourse that was less than, shall we say, civil. (See Figure 1.1.)

Since the definitions of *civil* and *discourse* were easy to find at merriam

Figure 1.1 - What Is *Civil Discourse*?

civ·il[1]: [('si-vəl) *adjective*]
2a: civilized <*civil* society\> **b:** adequate in courtesy and politeness; mannerly <a *civil* question>

dis·course: [('dis-ˌkōrs) *noun*]
2. verbal interchange of ideas; conversation

What will you do if . . . ?

The following scenarios from actual book clubs present some challenges to engaging in civil discourse. Talk them over as a way of figuring out in advance how you'll deal with them if they occur in your book club.

An event or idea arises in the text that is central to the story but might be considered controversial. Talking about it might make everyone uncomfortable. What will you do?

1. Someone asks a question that challenges your point of view. What will you do?

2. At the beginning of a book club discussion, someone says, "This book is so boring!" You thought it was interesting, but now you're afraid to disagree. What will you do?

3. One of your book club members sits silently through the entire discussion, but you know she's read the book. What will you do?

4. A book club member keeps trying to get everyone off-topic. What will you do?

5. Someone makes a sweeping generalization about a character's behavior that you consider inappropriate (for example, "all poor people are lazy" or "everyone who lives on an Indian reservation is an alcoholic"). What will you do?

6. A disagreement gets heated, and one book club member won't stop talking long enough to let the other person speak. What will you do?

7. You want to ask a question, but you're afraid everyone will think it's stupid. What will you do?

[1]Definitions from merriam-webster.com.

Tough Talk, Tough Texts

-webster.com, we used these words and their definitions as headings for the handout. Explaining our definition dilemma to the students, we asked for their help not just with *defining* the term civil discourse but in *enacting* it since the working definition the class created would shape the discussion norms they would use in their book clubs.

Although Rebecca and I saw the handout as a short-term fix, we've ultimately discovered how useful it is to allow students to generate a definition inductively that they will refine over the course of a civil discourse sequence (CDS), that is, the range of activities we use to prepare kids to discuss tough texts, sustain their conversations, and assess their work once they've finished the book. When students "own" the definition, they are more likely to use it to guide their work, so we still use the handout to this day and recommend the following procedures as the very first lesson in a CDS:

CDS: Lesson One

1. In small groups of three to five, ask students to consider each of the scenarios listed on the handout. In case students think that any of the events are far-fetched, explain that all of them have occurred in book club or small-group discussions. (You may want to replace some of these scenarios with others you've observed in your own classroom.)

2. Students should discuss each scenario and come up with solutions that their small group would consider reasonable. Groups should choose one person to serve as the *scribe*, recording their possible solutions on a sheet of paper, and another to serve as the *reporter* who will share the group's ideas with the whole class in subsequent discussion. An optional role is *discussion leader* to help keep the group's discussion on track.

3. After groups have completed their discussions (usually in about fifteen minutes), ask reporters to share their group's ideas with the rest of the class. As groups present, record their ideas on the board or project them using a document camera. Put tick marks beside solutions that get mentioned more than once.

4. Discuss these solutions either as you go or after all groups have reported. Encourage students to share the reasoning behind their solutions. Ask questions such as these: *Why is this a reasonable solution?*

Why do you think some solutions were mentioned more than once? Which solutions seem most likely to help you engage in productive small-group discussion? Why?

5. Ask students to record the solutions in their notes for future reference as they develop norms for their book clubs or small groups.

6. Conclude with this final question: *Based on our discussion, how are we defining the term* civil discourse *right now?* Consider the question orally as a class, or ask students to quickwrite in their journals. Either way, explain that they will revisit this question at various points over the next few weeks (e.g., when they set their book club or small-group norms, during their discussions, in their final projects).

Asking students to consider separate definitions for *civil* and *discourse* solved Rebecca's and my worksheet problem in the short term, but take another look at the definitions at the top of the handout:

civ·il: [('si-vəl) *adjective*]
2a: civilized <*civil* society> **b:** adequate in courtesy and politeness; mannerly <a *civil* question>

dis·course: [('dis-,kōrs) *noun*]
2: verbal interchange of ideas; conversation

These definitions worked fine as starting places to help the students begin thinking about the notion of civil discourse, but Rebecca and I knew that we were conceiving of civil discourse as more than the simple sum of these parts—as more than "mannerly conversation," in other words. This description seemed inadequate, connoting as it did a superficial exchange that never exceeded mere tolerance. From the beginning, we knew that we wanted to help students achieve something more than this as they took on the difficult issues emerging in the tough texts they were reading. We wanted to help them dig deep into these issues by engaging in tough talk—dialogue that was substantive, rigorous, and respectful.

Back in the university library with the *Oxford English Dictionary (OED)*, I found a gaping hole where the definition of civil discourse should have been, right between *civil defense* and *civil disobedience*, so I again resorted to looking for each word on its own. Pressuring the definitions of both *civil* and *discourse* as these appeared in the *OED* confirmed my suspicions that "mannerly conversation" was an insufficient synonym. One of the contemporary definitions for *civil* points out that while the term has in the past suggested polite or courteous behavior, even this definition is "sinking in recent use to 'decently polite,' 'up to the ordinary or minimum standard of courtesy,' or the merely negative sense of 'not (actually) rude'" (definition 12, *OED* print edition, 255). The civility Rebecca and I were hoping to foster among students related more to archaic or obsolete definitions of the word that were common during Shakespearean times, such as "well-ordered . . . well-governed" (definition 7, 255) or "humane, gentle, kind" (definition 11, 255).

The same held true for *discourse.* In the noun form of the word, one of today's prevailing definitions is "a spoken or written treatment of a subject, in which it is handled or discussed at length; a dissertation, treatise, homily, sermon, or the like" (definition 5, 751). Likewise, when used as a verb, the word means "to speak or write at length on a subject; to utter or pen a discourse" (definition 4, 751). These definitions suggested the kind of holding forth we wanted students to *avoid* in book clubs. Rather than coming to class with their minds already made up about a subject, we wanted them to explore the subject together through the informal conversation that is the hallmark of a good small-group discussion.

In the end, the etymology of *discourse* illuminates the kinds of exchanges we were after. The word originates in the Latin verb *discurs-us,* which means "running to and fro, conversation" (750). Again, the obsolete and archaic definitions were more apt for our purposes. The second definition listed for the noun form, for instance, describes *discourse* as "the faculty of reasoning, reason, rationality," offering this definition from *The Works of John Wesley* (1872): "Discourse, strictly speaking, is the motion or progress of the mind from one judgment to another."

The *OED* noted that Samuel Johnson's dictionary refers to *discourse* as "*mutual* intercourse of language" (definition 3, 751, emphasis mine). Useful archaic definitions in the verb sense include:

- "To turn over in the mind, think over." This definition cites Stefano Guazzo's *Civil Conversations* in saying "He discoursed many things in his minde" (definition 5b, 751).

- "To pass (time) away in discourse or talk; to bring (a person) by discourse into (some state)" (definition 3b, 751).

- "To go through in speech; to treat of in speech or writing; to talk over, discuss; to talk of, converse about; to tell, narrate, relate" (definition 5, 751).

Although archaic, these definitions more accurately describe the objective we hoped to help students reach as they engaged in civil discourse. We wanted conversations that were self-regulated, reasoned, and humane rather than driven by impulsive emotions or prior bias. We wanted there to be an exploratory quality to their investigation of the cultural issues at hand that might bring students into a state of openness, seeing things from another's point of view or even changing one's mind. And we wanted literacy practices like reading, writing, speaking, listening, and visualizing to be the vehicles by which students traveled "to and fro" among the possible perspectives on the topic or question arising in the literature at hand.

Our etymological journey sharpened Rebecca's and my focus, helping us better understand what we were after in helping students engage in civil discourse. Since then, we've learned, however, that even the amplified sum of these definitional parts doesn't capture what students are able to accomplish when they are properly prepared to discuss tough texts and supported in doing so. Rather, by observing numerous discussions in Rebecca's, Beth's, and Cam's classrooms, I've extrapolated a definition of civil discourse that more accurately captures the texture of students' interchanges as they discuss tough texts. Based on these observations, civil discourse is

- not just *tolerant of,* but *considerate of, intentionally empathic toward,* characters' and classmates' perspectives;

- culturally relevant, in that it involves grappling with real issues that exist both in and out of school;

- thoughtful, thought-provoking, and exploratory;

- catalytic, or capable of sparking a change in outlook or perspective on a complex social issue or, at the very least, a respectful acknowledgment that a range of perspectives exists;

- inclusive of that range of views; and thus

- gently radical.

Clearly, this amplified definition provides evidence of the immediate application of social justice principles as these play out in settings where tough talk is encouraged. In so many of the methods recommended by social justice approaches to teaching—and I applaud these practices as sound and worthy in their own right—concrete proof of students' application of social justice principles is delayed until the final project, when they submit an editorial to the local newspaper, build a playground for a women-and-children's shelter, or hold a canned food drive to raise awareness of hunger in a local community.

Not so in classrooms where engaging in civil discourse about culturally sensitive topics is one way of enacting social justice in and of itself. Speech act theorists have long argued that language use is itself a form of social action (e.g., Austin 1962; Searle 1969; Wittgenstein 1953). Thomas Holtgraves (2002) points out that

> to use language is to perform an action. It is an attempt to alter the world in some way . . . or to commit oneself to a particular depiction of the world . . . or to describe one's inner state. . . . Obviously one alters the world with declaratives (e.g., "I declare war on Ohio"). But all utterances are actions in the same sort of way, albeit on a much smaller scale. They are social actions—actions that are directed toward other people. (177–78)

Holtgraves also points out that our linguistic actions have implications for our relationships with others because "people are not abstract entities devoid of feelings, goals, thoughts, and values. People's language use—how they perform actions with language—must be sensitive to these concerns. . . . By attending to others' feelings we increase the likelihood that they will attend to ours" (5–6).

If we assume that students mean what they say in literature discussions—that they can listen with openness and frame what they say with their listeners' well-being in mind—then engaging in civil discourse requires a great deal of skill, attentiveness, and empathy. Such talk is not "cheap," for it is a deliberate and conscious choice—what some might even call a practice—to resist a priori thinking and raise the social consciousness of others through collaborative conversation.

Students' small-group interactions, their written work and final projects, and my interviews with them are saturated with proof that students as young as sixth graders are consciously able and willing to use civil discourse to tackle difficult issues in complex and substantive ways. I've observed Beth's, Cam's, and Rebecca's students thoughtfully considering the likelihood of peace, questioning the inevitability of war, pondering the influence of one's religious upbringing on attitudes toward sexuality, speculating about the potential impact of nonviolent resistance, wondering aloud about technology's sway on one's worldview, *and* doing so collaboratively without a teacher's prompting.

Students engaging in tough talk are enacting democracy by way of literacy. In the small space of a book club nested in the confines of a single classroom, they are thereby developing new *mind-sets* and *skill sets* that have the potential to be transferred to larger spaces in the much wider world (Wood, Bruner, and Ross 1976). They are discovering the great capacity of literacy as "a tool for improving the world they share, a means of making a better future" (Bomer 2007, 310).

What Are Tough Texts?

Tough talk is one thing, but it's nothing without tough texts to talk about. Even though you may have a sense of what a tough text is, you should be convinced by now that I really am a stickler for official definitions.

Tough texts set the stage for tough talk because they meet the following criteria:

- They treat culturally relevant and universally significant topics, issues, or questions complexly and incite engaging conversation about them.

- They include well-developed characters, often adolescents, whom students are likely to care about and connect with in some way because of the choices and challenges they face.

- They display high literary quality as determined by narrative structure, stylistic features, and/or external recognition, such as awards or outstanding reviews from reputable sources.

It's also no accident that many tough texts are written by authors of color and/or feature protagonists of color. Much has been written about expanding the traditional literary canon to include more multicultural texts, but in *Culturally Responsive Teaching*, Geneva Gay (2000) succinctly summarizes the benefits. She explains that multicultural literature is a powerful medium through which students can confront social injustices, visualize racial inequalities, find solutions to personal and political problems, and vicariously experience the issues, emotions, thoughts, and lives of people otherwise inaccessible to them. These literary encounters help students "become critical readers, who learn to view the world from multiple perspectives as they construct their versions of the truth, . . . [and] make informed and rational decisions about the most effective ways to correct injustices in their community" (Diamond and Moore, 1995, p. 14). (131)

Even young students are capable of taking this sort of sophisticated perspective when discussing a tough text if they find that it meets the first criterion on the above list, *cultural relevance*. In the classrooms I've observed, most students can project themselves into times, settings, and realities different from their own if the *issues* in the text really matter to them. Students deem texts relevant if they raise interesting questions worth exploring further in writing and discussion. Thus when selecting texts for a CDS, Beth, Cam, and Rebecca always ask themselves, *Could this text provoke interesting conversations about topics that might be culturally sensitive but are culturally crucial nonetheless?* If so, they keep it in the lineup. If not, they look for something that will.

Tough texts don't just raise controversial topics for controversy's sake, however; they also treat them in complex ways. Topics like religion, class, race, and gender move front and center because good stories demand tension, and tension is what these topics are all about. More important, though, tough texts meet the second criterion on the list by featuring *well-developed characters students can relate to*, who make these topics personal. When students see protagonists, usually adolescents, wrestling with difficult social, emotional, and moral choices and challenges that demand the exercising of values, they are also willing to examine these choices within the relatively safe space that literature provides.

Finally, these texts are "tough" in terms of their structural and stylistic sophistication. *High literary quality* is evident in the complexity with which the controversial topics are treated and the "roundness," or intellectual, emotional, and spiritual authenticity, characters demonstrate as they deal with them. Tough texts typically earn positive critical reviews, and many of their authors have won or have been nominated for literary awards that suggest their work will stand the test of time.

Now that we share a picture of the same elephant, let's examine why we ought to put these definitions of tough talk and tough text into practice. In the next chapter, you'll learn how texts that meet all three criteria—cultural relevance, relatable characters, and literary sophistication—can prompt students to contemplate worthwhile questions and issues that matter deeply to all of us as human beings and to confront them together using civil discourse, an enterprise that is well worth the effort you and your students will expend.

Chapter 2

Teaching students how to engage in civil discourse sounded like trouble waiting to happen, a teacher recently insisted at a workshop I led. Tough texts were too heavy and complex, too dark for young readers to deal with. Why focus on them intentionally, she wanted to know. Why not make classrooms a place where innocence is preserved rather than tested? Aren't students becoming too jaded already?

They might be in some instances, I acknowledged, but I also made the case that students' cynicism is not the result of difficult questions posed, but of difficult questions posed and then banished from conversation. Living with three adolescents under my own roof for the past ten years, I know that thorny issues are as much part and parcel of adolescent life today as they are a part of the larger world. Sweeping them out of the classroom rather than acknowledging that they exist does our students a disservice. Besides, the tough texts that I recommend in this book emphasize the great strength and resilience humans, especially adolescents, are capable of demonstrating in response to the challenges they face. Even when the characters in them are in great difficulty, these texts offer the sharp relief of hope. As Jerome Bruner put it, narratives "worth telling and worth construing are typically born in trouble" (1996, 142).

Rehearsals for Social Change
Why Teaching Tough Texts Is Worth the Trouble

The same might be said about some other tough texts we all hold dear. A recent exhibit at the Library of Congress, *Creating the United States*, provided a look at how the nation's founding documents were produced. Of all the documents, I was most fascinated to see the rough draft of the Constitution. Prior to seeing it, I'd never expected to see the words *rough draft* and *Constitution* in the same sentence. In fact I'd always imagined it being handed down from on high, much the way Moses received the Ten Commandments; but the manuscript showed evidence of hard labor. Thomas Jefferson's flowing hand was rife with strikethroughs. Carets indicated where to insert additional words and phrases. Brackets marked places where alternative wording might be in order. Comments and suggestions in the handwriting of Benjamin Franklin, John Adams, and other members of the Continental Congress appeared vertically in the margins.

Standing in front of the document, I imagined Thomas Jefferson handing the draft to Benjamin Franklin, who pored over it later that evening by lamplight, quill pen in hand. I could picture the negotiations that occurred the next day with Jefferson and his fellow writers as they painstakingly worded the principles that would guide a nation. Admittedly, my first thought when I saw the draft was "killer writing group"! On further reflection, however, I realized, as I never had before, that this textual evidence and the other documents that surround it reveal that the bedrock of our democracy was forged in grand conversation. In 1776 and many times since, tough talk about tough texts has indisputably changed the world. Although it's sometimes hard to see beyond all the baggy pants, disheveled hair, and lip gloss and imagine who our students will become, our nation's future leaders are sitting in someone's classroom at this very moment. Who's to say it isn't yours?

Kelly Gallagher cites literary theorist and philosopher Kenneth Burke's 1968 argument that the value in reading books for young people (and, I would argue, for all of us) lies in providing "imaginative rehearsals" for participating in the wider world. Using *To Kill a Mockingbird* as a case in point, Gallagher argues:

> Reading and discussing Lee's novel enables students to make connections between the issues illustrated in the novel and the issues found in their world. It gives them the opportunity to read, to write, and to argue about these issues in a modern context. We do not want our students only to read stories; we want them to read novels to make

them wiser about the world. We want to take advantage of the imaginative rehearsals that great literature provides before our students reach adulthood. (2009, 69)

I firmly believe that teaching tough texts *is* worth the trouble. In addition to acknowledging questions and issues many adolescents are likely to face in their own lives, tough texts offer many other benefits for adolescent readers. They stretch students intellectually and teach them to forge empathic connections with texts and one another that also have consequences for the culture at large. In other words, tough texts not only allow the imaginative rehearsals Burke and Gallagher describe as possible, but they also allow students to engage in civil discourse to create a more socially just world.

The Academic Benefits of Reading and Responding to Tough Texts

Time and again, reluctant readers, especially in high school, have told me that the tough text they just finished was the first (and best) book that they had read in years or perhaps ever. A few years back, six boys reading *The Perks of Being a Wallflower* (Chbosky 1999) in Beth's alternative high school class told me at their second book club meeting that they were struggling not to abandon the reading schedule they had agreed to, not because they fell behind but because they couldn't put the book down. One of the boys, Gerald, who later told Beth that *Perks* was the first book he had read in four years, began the discussion that day by telling the group that he had to hide the book under a pile of clothes in his room the night before so that he could get the rest of his homework done.

Beth and I had feared this group might have trouble staying on task, but our fears proved unfounded. Instead, the boys routinely wowed us by demonstrating the moves of sophisticated readers. They discussed the plot, yes, but they also read closely, analyzed character believability and the author's stylistic techniques, made connections to their own experiences, and used the book as a lens for critiquing adolescent culture and exploring cultural issues. In one discussion, they astutely analyzed Charlie, the main character of *Perks*, as well as tackling a range of topics as wide as homosexuality, the nature of truth, the effect of first-person point of view on the narrator's relationship with the reader, and the question of whether or not conventional science is primarily descriptive or theoretical—all in the span of a half-hour discussion, mind you, *and* they did so without leaving the book behind.

Because it's impossible to examine a facilely constructed book in such a manner, this anecdote should make clear that one of the academic benefits of reading tough texts is immersion in literary quality. An added and not inconsequential bonus is that kids will willingly read them (or devour them, in the case of Gerald's book club). I've seen this phenomenon recur countless times over the years in Cam's and Rebecca's classrooms as well, and I believe I know why. Despite the challenging nature of tough texts and their inclusion of culturally sensitive topics, they often feature young narrators like Charlie and his friends with whom students are likely to connect.

It's no accident that many of these books are young adult texts. Young adult (YA) literature has suffered a bad rap over the years, sometimes seen as inferior in quality to classic literature. Even though these criticisms were arguably justifiable at one time, the literary complexity of YA literature overall has increased dramatically in the past couple of decades at the same time that its subject matter has remained compelling. Since the 1980s, plots have grown more reliably complex, the structures more experimental, the settings more realistic, and the characters more layered. Betty Carter comments that today's YA literature consists of "sophisticated, edgy books about issues that reflect today's more complex society and culture" (2000, 9), and Teri Lesesne points out that the "new YA literature tests kids' mettle as it pushes them to think critically and respond personally" (2007, 63). When we assign YA texts, then, we can be confident of the academic benefits they confer. (Notable exceptions include series books like Goosebumps and Gossip Girl, which might be fine for recreational reading but are too facile to make the cut as tough texts.)

It would be a mistake to limit tough texts to YA literature, however. Even though all YA literature features adolescents in prominent roles, all books with adolescent characters are not considered YA literature. The area between YA and more mainstream fiction has become increasingly gray. Consider *Sky Bridge*, by Laura Pritchett, for instance, another book Beth Lewis's high school students read in book clubs. The novel tells the story of Libby, a young woman who decides to adopt her sister Tess's newborn daughter when Tess skips town a few days after giving birth. Although *Sky Bridge* was a Top Ten Pick for *School Library Journal*, it also received a WILLA Award in the category of contemporary fiction for adults. Named after Willa Cather, the WILLA honors outstanding stories that feature women and that are set in the West. Pritchett did not, however, write the book with a young adult audience in mind (personal conversation, 2008).

When I asked Laura what she made of the fact that she had apparently written a crossover book, she said that in some ways she was not surprised. After all, coming-of-age stories like Salinger's *Franny and Zooey* have appealed to both adult and young adult audiences for some time. As our conversation continued, however, we came to the conclusion that *Sky Bridge*, like other tough texts, defies the traditional coming-of-age label. For although the main characters are definitely headed somewhere developmentally by the end of the book, they haven't arrived yet. We speculated that this is perhaps because one typically comes of age not just once during adolescence but several times over in the course of growing up in our culture. In contemporary life, multiple rites of passage exist. Likewise, in tough texts, while the main character's outlook has definitely changed by the conclusion of the book, readers are unlikely to find any neat-and-tidy resolution. In its place more often than not is the *hope* that one will eventually occur.

Because Laura lives near Beth's school, we were able to invite her to be a guest speaker in Beth's class near the end of one semester. Her discussion with the students confirmed that tough texts eschew a formulaic structure in favor of literary complexity sans the easy ending. In the case of *Sky Bridge*, Laura explained that this unfinished sense at the end of the novel made it feel true to her when she wrote it, rather than "sappy like a Hallmark card." While life does not always have a happy ending, she said, "Things can get better. But in real life, you have to fight for them to get better like Libby did."

Hannah, one of the girls who had read *Sky Bridge* in Beth's class, told Laura that this was the very thing that kept her up reading all night until she finished the book: "After what happened to Libby [she is the victim of date rape], I just couldn't leave her there. I had to get to something hopeful." Another student, Carter, chimed in about a similar theme in *The Perks of Being a Wallflower*, observing that "even when lots of bad things happen, you just have to move on."

Whether we look for tough texts within or beyond the field of YA literature, we have lots of choices. As long as the texts we're considering feature adolescent characters with whom we suspect our students will connect and are of high literary quality, we can choose from among those written specifically for young readers (e.g., *Heaven, The Bridge to Terabithia, Looking for Alaska*); books written about them but aimed more generally at adult readers (e.g., *Life of Pi, The*

Curious Incident of the Dog in the Nighttime); and books the authors themselves are reluctant to categorize (e.g., *The Golden Compass, Postcards from No Man's Land*). Recently, as I was browsing in an airport bookstore, I noticed that *The Perks of Being a Wallflower* was shelved in both adult and YA fiction; the same was true for both the *Golden Compass* and Hunger Games series. This crossover between YA literature and mainstream fiction is good news for us as teachers because it allows us not only to widen our search for tough texts but also to select texts that up the academic ante: students are guaranteed to encounter subtleties of style, nuanced characters, and plots with believable though often ambiguous endings. As a result, as Laura Pritchett noted with *Sky Bridge*, a chief characteristic of tough texts is that they "read true."

Another good example of a book that reads true is *Looking for Alaska*, John Green's 2005 story of the awkward young narrator Pudge's experiences in an Alabama boarding school. Among other things, these experiences include underage drinking and smoking, sex, the capacity of religion to address life's most difficult questions, class conflict, and death. Two of the most difficult topics that Green addresses in the book, however, are drunk driving and suicide. While the book does show the tragic consequences that can result when adolescents engage in risky behavior, Green comes across as anything but trite. Rather, we identify with Pudge as he deals with the glorious "before" of being accepted in a circle of friends for the first time in his life, and we suffer with him as he searches for answers in the ambiguous "after" following his friend's death. Green actually titles the first half of the book "Before" and the second half "After," thus structurally reinforcing the messy impact of life-changing events. Pudge's journey is a struggle that is funny, poignant, and heart-wrenching by turns. Ultimately, *Looking for Alaska* is simultaneously hopeful and realistic.

Over the years, Beth, Cam, and Rebecca have used the following titles as a natural inroad into teaching students how to become more accomplished readers of challenging books:

Tough Texts in Cam's Sixth-Grade Class
Almond, David. *Skellig.*
Johnson, Angela. *Heaven.*
Lowry, Lois. *The Giver.*
Lowry, Lois. *Gathering Blue.*

Paterson, Katherine. *Bridge to Terabithia*.

Philbrick, Rodman. *The Last Book in the Universe*.

Spinelli, Jerry. *Loser*.

Spinelli, Jerry. *Wringer*.

Tough Texts in Rebecca's Tenth-Grade Pre-AP English Class

Alvarez, Julia. *In the Time of the Butterflies*.

Anderson, M. T. *Feed*.

Chambers, Aidan. *Postcards from No Man's Land*.

Haddon, Mark. *The Curious Incident of the Dog in the Nighttime*.

Martel, Yann. *Life of Pi*.

Paton, Alan. *Cry the Beloved Country*.

Pullman, Philip. *The Golden Compass*.

Rosoff, Meg. *How I Live Now*.

Stratton, Allan. *Chanda's Secrets*.

Vijayaraghavan, Vineeta. *Motherland*.

Tough Texts in Beth's Multiage High School English Class

Alexie, Sherman. *The Absolutely True Diary of a Part-Time Indian*.

Anderson, M. T. *Feed*.

Chbosky, Steven. *The Perks of Being a Wallflower*.

Evslin, Bernard. *Heroes, Gods, and Monsters of the Greek Myths*.

Green, John. *Looking for Alaska*.

Mikaelsen, Ben. *Touching Spirit Bear*.

Porter, Connie. *Imani All Mine*.

Pritchett, Laura. *Sky Bridge*.

Salinger, J. D. *Catcher in the Rye*.

It's not just the literary quality of tough texts like these that confer academic benefits; it's also what you teach students to do with them. In a typical civil discourse sequence (CDS), students will write a great deal, critique literary quality, use technology, and compose sophisticated multimodal interpretations of texts, all the while engaging in civil discourse. Beth refers to this combination of response strategies and assignments as "sneaky teaching" because it allows teachers to provide support as needed without "killing the books" in the process. As a result, students are able to dig into complex texts and generate well-developed interpretations that both synthesize and build on their responses over time.

In so doing, students practice critical thinking, as Freire describes it, moving far beyond mere skill acquisition to "the development of critical curiosity and thought" (2004, 93).

The Emotional and Social Benefits of Reading and Responding to Tough Texts

In addition to helping students grow academically, tough texts also contribute to their emotional and social development. Monique, one of Beth's students, demonstrates the emotional impact of Connie Porter's book *Imani All Mine* when she talks about the main character, Tasha, who is an African American teenage mother:

> For some reason reading about it and actually getting attached to the character and learning the character and everything, it's a lot harder. . . . In real life you just see it, and you just see the aftermath. You don't see how their life was before and how it affects them and devastates them. You just see, oh well, somebody got killed. You don't feel that emotion from it because you don't personally know them, and you don't personally know their mind and everything like that.

Monique's comments make it clear that even though she is white and lives nowhere near the inner city, this tough text has helped her read with empathy. In fact, she claims to have a stronger reaction to the tragic events that befall Tasha, the fictional African American, than she has to many real-life events. Having "known the mind" of Tasha through reading, Monique talks about her as if she is real, saying "I was so mad at her, so frustrated" when Tasha becomes pregnant again at the end of the book after her daughter Imani is killed in a drive-by shooting.

Monique's response confirms Robert Coles's claim that novels can remind students of "life's contingencies; and in so doing, they take matters of choice and commitment more seriously than they might otherwise have done" (1989, 90). This is exactly why Monique found the endings of both *Imani All Mind* and *Looking for Alaska* frustrating—not because she found them unrealistic but because they were "so devastating, so hard to read." Yet she framed her emotional involvement as "the sign of a good book" and insisted that both books were good book club choices for students who are "mature enough to read them."

Psychologist and novelist Keith Oatley provides insight into why books like *Imani All Mine* can help students like Monique develop the practice of empathy. Oatley draws on recent brain research and a study analyzing adults' responses to films to show the capacity for art to prompt the empathy for which the human brain is hardwired. He claims that in addition to identifying on a basic level with characters in fiction and films,

> we can start to extend ourselves into situations we have never experienced, feel for people very different from ourselves, and begin to understand such people in ways we may never have thought possible. . . . [A]rt is capable of inducing one of the most profound aspects of empathy: the ability to sensitize us to the emotions of other people, transcending the limits of our own experiences and perspectives. (2005, 14)

Oatley's insights explain why Monique and so many other students from Beth's, Cam's, and Rebecca's classrooms made similarly intense connections to characters in the tough texts they were reading. Regardless of how different the characters' circumstances are from their own, students formed intense emotional bonds with them. Something resonated, and they were able to "take the books to heart" (Coles 1989, 63).

As a result, students like Monique often inadvertently develop new communities of readers by encouraging others to read the books they have loved. Monique's book club members, as well as other students in Beth's class, had such enthusiastic responses to their tough texts, they even recommended them to their teachers. Beth said that in her many years of teaching, she has never had faculty members knocking on her door to check out books that kids were recommending. Since the word has gotten around, these books have become part of an unofficial canon at Beth's school, and students throughout the school now belong to an informal community of readers. Because many students new to Beth's class have already read *Imani All Mine* and other tough texts from her curriculum based entirely on word-of-mouth recommendations from their peers, they have charged her with finding some more books that are "just as good, but that we haven't read yet." Good problem.

Monique's willingness to recommend *Imani All Mine* to others arose from the book's ability to help her see a world that contrasted with her own through the main character Tasha's eyes. The response strategies Monique learned in tandem with *Imani All Mine* helped her to respond to Tasha and to her peers who were also reading the book in empathic ways, even when they didn't see eye-to-eye. She summed up her reaction to her book club experience by saying that "even though the book is kind of disheartening, you know it kind of hurts to read it a little bit, it does open your eyes to a different perspective, and it's definitely pretty nice to read."

Monique's comments demonstrate how tough texts enable readers to have the *doubly dialogic* experience of measuring their own take on controversial issues against others' perspectives, both those of the book's characters and those of their peers. Numerous theorists, including Rosenblatt, Vygotsky, Bakhtin, and Freire, have commented on the dialogic nature of engaged reading that requires the reader to forge a temporary relationship with the author. Because this relationship is a conversation of sorts, the author's voice matters. That is, the reader must heed Rosenblatt's (1978/1994) warning not to leave the text behind and get lost in one's own reactions to it. Freire likewise advises the reader to make "a determined effort not to betray the author's spirit" (1998, 30). Dialogue with an author's rendering of a text can thus result in "perceptive encounters . . . [that] can bring human beings in touch with themselves" (Greene 1977, 124).

Because other points of view can function as additional "texts" for consideration, tough talk enables a *doubly dialogic* experience by extending the author-reader conversation to fellow readers as well. Freire emphasizes

> the need for reading . . . as a dialogic experience in which the discussion of the text undertaken by different readers clarifies, enlightens, and creates group comprehension of what has been read. Deep down, group reading brings about the emergence of different *points of view* that, as they become exposed to each other, enrich the production of text comprehension. (1998, 30)

By reading tough texts, students learn to grapple personally with subjects, themes, and issues that figure large in characters' lives as well as our contemporary culture. By discussing tough texts, they also figure out how to engage in civil discourse—that is, to consider the perspectives of their peers in respectful, productive ways. In a very real sense, then, reading tough texts is an activity that is perhaps best tried in the company of others, because it requires that students move beyond the "closed circle of their own minds" (Freire 1998, 10).

Forging empathic connections with texts and peers undoubtedly provides social and emotional benefits for students, but recent work has suggested that these sophisticated moves also help them grow intellectually. In *Understanding by Design*, Grant Wiggins and Jay McTighe include empathy as one of the six facets of understanding along with explanation, interpretation, application, perspective, and self-knowledge. They explain that empathy

> is not simply an affective response or sympathy over which we have little control, but the disciplined attempt to feel as others feel, to see as others see. . . . [I]ntellectual empathy is essential if we are to make sense of ideas that we too quickly reject because of our assumptions. All scholars need empathy. (2005, 98–99)

Likewise, Ellin Oliver Keene (2008) identifies empathy as one of the key outcomes of deep understanding and describes various cognitive strategies to help students experience empathy for literary characters, settings, conflicts, authors, and in general.

I have no doubt that you've experienced empathy as a reader (otherwise, you wouldn't be an English teacher), so you probably have a good understanding of it as an individual, internal process. You may be less clear, however, about what empathic reading looks like in small-group discussion, so I want to offer an example from Cameron's sixth-grade classroom. You'll remember from Chapter 1 that Cam teaches in Belton Plains, a rural community known for its ideological conservatism. During one book club, his students tackled the topic of religion as prompted by their reaction to Katherine Paterson's novel *The Bridge to Terabithia*.

The group was discussing the chapter "Easter," in which Leslie, one of the book's central characters, reflects on her first time attending her friend Jess's church. Unlike Jess and his sisters, Leslie doesn't view the Bible as literally true, instead seeing the account of Jesus's death and resurrection as a "kind of beautiful story—like Abraham Lincoln or Socrates—or Aslan" of the *Chronicles of Narnia* (Paterson 1977/1987, 84). When one of Cam's students said that she saw the Bible as Leslie did because that was how she had been brought up at home, the other book club members were as shocked as Jess and his sisters. Initially, they clammed up, until Cam, who happened to be walking by about that time and overheard the discussion, dropped in on the group briefly and asked, "So what are you going to do about the elephant in the room?" Silence. Cam gently prompted the students to refer to their book club norms to remind themselves about how they had decided to deal with difficult topics, and then he moved on to listen in other groups.

After reviewing their norms together (and undoubtedly screwing up their courage), the other students in the book club also described how their respective upbringings had influenced their views on the Bible and religion in general. The contributions made by one of the students, an English language learner named Jaime, were especially interesting. On one of my previous visits to the classroom, Cam had explained that he would be especially curious to see how Jaime participated in book clubs. Although bright and capable, and despite Cam's encouragement, Jaime was reluctant to take part in whole-class discussions because he was self-conscious about making a verbal mistake. During book clubs, Cameron was pleased to notice that Jaime participated far more than he did in discussions undertaken by the whole class.

On the day religion came up, the group had chosen Jaime to be the scribe in charge of summarizing the discussion with other students' input and recording it on the discussion record (see Chapter 5) they would turn in to Cam.[1] Jaime summed up the book club's conversation as follows:

> *The cherectors talked about the bibl and what it said. Riligin is controver-*
> *sial and people biliv in what thay biliv. We talked about what we bilived.*

Like countless scholars and theologians before them, these sixth graders were unable to reach a consensus on their religious views. Nor was consensus the point. Rather, by reading empathically and intersecting their own cultural perspectives with the culture of the book, the students were able to arrive at an enlarged understanding of the issue at hand. Furthermore, all of the students, including Jaime, were able to listen carefully, speak respectfully to one another, and reflect on the group's complex reactions to a culturally sensitive topic. Their access to civil discourse strategies allowed them to explore and negotiate various perspectives, in both literature and their book club, that resembled or differed from their own. They indeed demonstrated a civil approach to problem solving, one with limitless opportunities for application in similar circumstances outside the classroom.

---

[1] Jaime's inventive spelling reflects the wider berth for conventional correctness that Cam allows on "first-draft finals" (Atwell 2007) like the discussion record. At Cam's request, I'm including Jaime's response, letter for letter and word for word.

The Cultural Benefits of Reading Tough Texts

Sharon Bishop reminds us that "if we teach students to live well in one place, they will transfer that knowledge to a new place" (2003, 82). The examples from Monique, Jaime, and the other students I described above point directly to the academic, emotional, and social benefits of reading tough texts within the classroom, but scholars have also described how certain books can influence students' beliefs and actions beyond the classroom. Drawing on a number of titles that have been historically significant to African American males, for instance, Alfred Tatum defines an *enabling text* as "one that moves beyond a sole cognitive focus, such as skill and strategy development, to include a social, cultural, political, spiritual, or economic focus" (2006, 47). Within the context of culturally responsive teaching, such texts enable students "in some way to be, do, or think differently as a result of the texts" (13). Lisa Habegger adds that "[t]he power of these books to create controversy can also be emblematic of their power to create change and to have an impact on adolescent lives" (2004, 39).

Likewise in *The Call of Stories: Teaching and the Moral Imagination*, Robert Coles explores the lasting cultural impact that certain texts can have on young adult readers. Coles reports on interviews conducted with students in his wife's high school English class in Georgia during the sixties, shortly after school desegregation. Although the school had been proactive in trying to help students deal with prejudicial attitudes by showing them documentaries and providing lectures by sociologists, the students found these efforts to be largely irrelevant. What made more of an impression, however, was students' reading and discussion of stories by Tillie Olson. In this school and others, students authentically engaged the social and personal issues they faced daily in school and many other personal issues besides, such as racism, alcoholism and family dynamics, social order, and identity. Coles attributes this more lasting impact to the power of stories to "address . . . life's burdens indirectly and directly" through the characters' perspectives and circumstances (1989, 62).

Why did the less didactic approach that literature provides have cultural consequences on the Georgia students beyond the particular instance of reading? As Coles explains:

> . . . Tillie Olson didn't come to them with her finger wagging or with a list of formulations they could readily ignore. Her stories worked their way into the everyday reality of their young lives: watching their

mothers iron, and thinking of a story; watching a certain heavy-drink-
ing friend, relative, neighbor, and thinking of a story; watching children in church, and themselves in school, and thinking of a story. (57)

Coles argues that when students let themselves "settle in" with a story, they not
only experience vicariously the characters' perspectives, circumstances, conflicts, and challenges but also call up parallel issues and events in their lives and
the larger culture; in other words, readers experience a "kind of moral com-
munion" (65).

In the Georgia case, talking through divisive cultural issues with the help of a
literary text, what Parker Palmer (2004) refers to as a "third thing," also gave students the distance they temporarily needed to sort through the controversies
they were facing daily in the outside world. Judging by this example, tough texts
allow readers to evoke a context without directly participating in it, to invest in
characters without meeting them face-to-face, and to confront cultural controversy without personalizing it. Paradoxically, the empathic connection readers
forge feels intimate at the same time that it is distanced.

As Cameron's sixth graders' discussion about religion illustrates and Coles's
commentary suggests, a tough text can function as a bridge where students feel
safe to meet and engage in civil discourse. An individual reader can ponder the
culturally sensitive issues contained in tough texts and then slide the book back
on the shelf. When discussing books with their peers, however, students who
engage in civil discourse on these same issues come to recognize that "[w]hether
we know it or not, like it or not, acknowledge it or not, our lives are intercon-
nected in a complex web of causation. My understanding of truth impinges on
your life, and yours impinges on mine, so the differences between us matter to
both of us" (Palmer 2004, 126–27).

Engaging in civil discourse about tough texts simultaneously matters in the
moment and functions as practice for life outside school. Thus in the process of
working through their and others' reactions to racism (or any other difficult
issue) as it occurs in a tough text, students are able to confront the reality of
racism as it exists in their lives beyond the classroom. Maxine Greene explains
that by engaging with literature and other art forms, we are urged "[to] see more,
to hear more. By such experiences we are not only lurched out of the familiar
and the taken-for-granted, but we may also discover new avenues for action. We
may experience a sudden sense of new possibilities and thus new beginnings"

(1995, 379). Likewise, Keith Oatley insists that books like tough texts can have cultural consequences beyond the reader:

> In literature we feel the pain of the downtrodden, the anguish of defeat, or the joy of victory—but in a safe space. In this space, we can, as it were, practice empathy. We can refine our human capacities of emotional understanding. We can hone our ability to feel with other people who, in ordinary life, might seem too foreign—or too threatening—to elicit our sympathies. Perhaps, then, when we return to our real lives, we can better understand why people act the way they do, and react with caution, even compassion toward them. (2005, 15)

To sum up, here's why teaching tough texts is worth the trouble: because if students are able to use civil discourse to engage in the "imaginative rehearsals" that literature provides, they will reap a host of academic, emotional, social, and cultural benefits. At the same time that they are becoming more motivated, proficient, and critical readers, they are also learning to view both the characters they read and the classmates with whom they interact more compassionately. By using enabling texts to recognize their own humanity and treat others accordingly, students can tackle pressing social issues, one book and one discussion at a time.

If all of this can happen—and I've seen it happen—then we teachers ought to heed Margaret Wheatley's advice in the epigraph that opened this chapter. We cannot underestimate the power of human conversation, even and especially when had by students, for these conversations just might change the world.

Chapter 3

To choose a good book, look in an inquisitor's prohibited list.

—JOHN AIKIN

Imagine that you wander up to the information desk at Barnes & Noble and the clerk asks whether he can help you find something. "Well, yes," you say, "I'm looking for a tough text for my classroom."

"Ah," he says, "a tough text, did you say?"

"Yes, that's it—a tough text."

"That's a title, I presume." He taps away at his computer.

"No, not exactly. It's more like . . . a category. You know, of books . . . that bring about social change."

The clerk nods his head slowly and taps away again on his keyboard. "Hmm, well, nothing here," he smiles, "but I'm sure we can find exactly what you're looking for."

He strides confidently down the aisle past Pets, Religion, and Self-Help until he gets to the Ts. He stops, scans the shelf, scratches his head. "Well, that's funny, now, isn't it? Here's Travel and True Crime, but no Tough Texts. I guess you're on your own."

Choosing Tough Texts for Your Classroom

While it's true that you won't find tough texts sitting in Barnes & Noble on a neatly labeled shelf, rest assured that you're not on your own when it comes to finding them or addressing the concerns of parents who might object to your teaching them.

How to Know a Tough Text When You See One

Using the criteria for a tough text identified in Chapter 1, I have created a one-page heuristic to help you decide which books should make the cut (see Appendix A-1, Is This Book a Tough Text?). I've grouped the questions on the heuristic into six broad categories: essential issues; cultural contexts; characters; choices, challenges, and resolutions; student appeal; and literary merit. You should be able to answer yes to most of the questions within each category in order to consider a book a tough text.

Essential Issues

Michael Smith and Jeff Wilhelm (2006) urge teachers to consider what is worth understanding and worth remembering beyond their classroom as they determine the concepts, strategies, and texts they will feature in their curriculum. As an example, Wilhelm explains that he taught *The Incredible Journey* to his students year after year "because it speaks to something that is of importance to humanity, something that we care about, something that is of great significance in our lives" (58); in other words, the text focuses on essential issues.

As you seek out tough texts that are worth caring about, keep these questions in mind:

- Does this book focus on significant issues that my students are likely to see as relevant?

- Are these issues treated in complex ways? In other words, does the book raise questions about these issues that prompt contemplation rather than encourage easy answers?

In her terrific book-length study *Adolescents Talk About Reading* (2004), Anne Reeves suggests that even though adolescents' interests vary widely, they share an interest in the following fundamental questions as they read:

- How do I become the adult I want to be, living the life I want to live, in the face of the obstacles I see?

- How do I relate to others to get what I want? Do I dominate, submit, or negotiate?

- How do I deal with the fact that I feel in some ways as if I do not fit into my culture?

- How do I meet the demands of my culture so I can fit in but also be true to myself? (254)

By posing difficult questions like these, tough texts address essential issues head-on, but what makes them worth understanding and remembering—and thus worth teaching—is the *way* they deal with these issues. In other words, just because a book deals with teenage suicide doesn't mean it qualifies as a tough text. To be sure, suicide is an essential issue for adolescent readers in particular to consider, but as you determine whether a book that focuses on this or any other tough topic is worth including in your curriculum, you have to ask yourself whether the book "reads true," as I discussed in the previous chapter. That is, does the author treat the topic in thought-provoking rather than didactic or gratuitously provocative ways? If your answer is yes, it's probably a tough text worth understanding and remembering.

Cultural Contexts

A few years ago, a friend asked me why I believed literature should be taught. The answers have always seemed so self-evident to me, I expected her next question to be something along the lines of why we should breathe. If I'd had the presence of mind to think of it, I might have used Muriel Rukeyser's notion that "the universe is made up of stories, not of atoms," but we had just returned from a hike to a mountain lake, and I was tired. Because this friend home-schools, I knew she was thinking ahead to how she and her daughter would spend their time in the coming year. What part, if any, should the study of literature play? If the point was helping her daughter learn to read well, why not just teach more practical or didactic books—textbooks or newspapers or even the Bible?

I thought for a moment and decided to answer as a mother instead of a professor. I explained that while practical texts are important, I want my own children to learn about literature in school for the same reason I read it, for the same reason we had told and listened to each other's stories all day long on our hike—so that they can make sense of their lives by "listening in" as literary characters make sense of theirs.

Tough texts can pry back our cultural filters, allowing us to eavesdrop on other worlds without physically leaving our own. They help us avoid the danger of seeing our worldview as *the* worldview. If we choose books that let students live vicariously through other worlds and teach them to read with empathy, we can help students avoid the same trap. That's why we should keep these questions in mind as we determine whether a book is a tough text:

- Knowing that students ultimately set their own purposes for reading, does this book—and/or students' discussion of it—have the potential to challenge or expand students' existing worldviews?

- Might it help them look at different cultural contexts from a variety of perspectives and in empathic ways?

Teachers from the UCLA Writing Project have created a useful continuum to help them think about how their own feelings about cultural issues influence the kinds of literature they elect to teach and the conversations they foster (or don't) around these issues in their classrooms (Carter, Mota-Altman, and Peitzman 2009). Though originally created in the context of a study group on the experiences of gay, lesbian, bisexual, and transgender (GLBT) teens in schools, I've broadened the continuum to address a range of important issues in various cultural contexts, including GLBT issues. I'm also referring to "culture" in a broader sense than that pertaining to race.

| I strongly and openly resist this cultural issue (e.g., homosexuality, race, class, religion, politics) if it arises in conversations with students and colleagues. | Discussing this cultural issue makes me feel personally uncomfortable. If I overhear students making disparaging comments in regard to this issue (e.g., "that's so gay"), I pretend not to notice. | I don't intentionally bring up this cultural issue in my classroom, but if conflicts around it arise, I take advantage of "teachable moments" and facilitate dialogue with students. | I intentionally introduce dialogue around this cultural issue into my classroom. I choose to teach texts that address this issue rather than having a one-time discussion about it. |

Figure 3.1 - Considering Cultural Issues in the Classroom: Where Do I Stand?

(based on work by teachers from the UCLA Writing Project study group on GLBT issues in schools)

We teachers sometimes joke about how little power we wield in the educational system, but as this continuum makes clear, we do have some say about what books we choose to teach and whether dialogue about the cultural issues contained within them has a place in our classroom. The ideas of the UCLA Writing Project study group represented in this continuum have made me think hard about teachers' agency in this regard. The continuum challenges us to use our power deliberately and wisely, to take seriously my friend's question "why teach literature?" I think it can

Tough Talk, Tough Texts

help you think hard, too, about whether a given book will help students grapple with cultural issues, giving them the chance to view the world from a variety of perspectives and in empathic ways.

Characters

"Making the match between book and reader relies on knowledge in three areas: knowing the reader, knowing the book, and knowing the techniques and strategies for bringing book and reader together," according to Teri Lesesne (2003, 1). Even though there's sometimes no accounting for taste, if we can make educated guesses about the characters our students will connect with, we're far more likely to select tough texts that will help make the match. These questions can help:

- Is the narrator or protagonist, preferably an adolescent, someone with whom my students will connect, even if she or he may differ from them in significant ways (e.g., race, class, gender, background)?

- Will my students care about these characters?

- Are characters well developed rather than stereotypical?

While Lesesne insists that "there is no one template for a reader" (2003, 31), some have speculated that adolescents progress sequentially through developmental stages of literary appreciation. Originating in ideas proposed by Margaret Early (1960), the following model of literary appreciation was later expanded by G. Robert Carlsen in *Books and the Teenage Reader* (1967/1980):

1. Reading for unconscious delight (in order to get lost in a book)

2. Reading for identification (in order to relate to characters like themselves and experiences and settings similar to their own)

3. Reading for vicarious experiences (in order to live through characters unlike themselves and experiences and settings unlike their own)

4. Reading for philosophical speculation (in order to contemplate big questions)

5. Reading for aesthetic experience (in order to feel the sheer joy of wallowing in words)

Carlsen's model can help us choose tough texts featuring characters who will meet students where they are because he based it on categories of the central developmental tasks students typically face in their teenage years, like relating to others, understanding the self, and making vocational choices. He suggests that because YA literature includes characters taking on these tasks, it holds great potential for meeting the needs of teenage readers. Pamela Sissi Carroll (1997) also recommends award-winning YA titles that feature characters wrestling with these changes, but she reviews more recent psychological studies that show how the developmental tasks today's adolescents typically face have expanded with cultural changes (a rise in divorce, increased teen poverty, changing sexual mores, and so on) in ways Carlsen could not have anticipated (Esman 1990; Heaven 1994).

Both Carlsen and Early insist that students must progress through each stage of literary appreciation sequentially. Early (1960) went so far as to say that only the most sophisticated readers ("teachers, critics, and writers," 167) will ever reach the final stage of aesthetic appreciation. I prefer to think of the boundaries between the stages as porous rather than hierarchical, however, because I've observed many instances when the stages don't correspond neatly with students' ages. With the support of more experienced readers and teachers like Beth, Cam, and Rebecca, I've seen even very young readers defy the stage model by speculating philosophically about the big questions faced by characters and appreciating the aesthetic elements of tough texts.

All of the students in a book club in Cameron's sixth-grade classroom, for instance, demonstrated *unconscious delight* in reading *The Golden Compass* (Pullman 1995), allowing themselves to get lost in the action of the book from the very first chapter. Their written responses and discussion also indicated that some students *identified* with the main character, Lyra, as a girl close to their age and wondered aloud what they'd do if they were in her shoes. Other students clearly enjoyed the chance to visit *vicariously* a world unlike their own, a world with armored bears and good witches. They excitedly imagined what animals their daemons (soul mates in the form of animals) would be if they were able to have them. Initially baffled by why the book would be banned, they also engaged in *philosophical speculation* during their discussions, reasoning that Pullman's upended system of good and evil might offend some readers who weren't used to seeing witches as more positive figures than church leaders. Perhaps because Cameron emphasized throughout the school year that they view books as mentor texts whose language they might appreciate as readers and emulate as writers, students also independently expressed their *aesthetic appreciation* for Pullman's language in their written responses. In responding to many elements of literary appreciation at once, then, they read far beyond their years.

Rebecca's tenth graders, also reading *The Golden Compass*, demonstrated all the same moves as the sixth graders did, at one point even jumping up in class to act out the battle of the armored bears. The tenth graders' spirited book club discussions, however, were dominated by *philosophical speculation* as they considered Pullman's critique of organized religion by way of Lyra and her altercations with other characters. They also read entire passages from the book aloud, expressing aesthetic appreciation of Pullman's language, closely examining his revision of biblical narratives (the creation story in Genesis, for example), and debating the doctrine of original sin.

Relevant to our discussion here, both Cam's and Rebecca's students experienced the elements (or stages, if you must) of literary appreciation *by way of the character Lyra*. In her case studies of adolescent readers, Anne Reeves (2004) also found that character identification was key to students' enjoyment of books. Reeves makes it clear that the high school readers she interviewed also experienced many elements of literary appreciation simultaneously when they read about characters worth caring about:

> When stating what they like, students mentioned stories about people like themselves or about characters with whom they can identify—and they were quick to say that they can identify with a character of a different gender or race as long as they can identify with what the character is experiencing. When the story catches the imagination, the student enjoys being in that world, working on the challenges the character is tackling. (240)

Early's and Carlsen's theories and Reeves's and my research make it clear that students come to appreciate literature by way of characters. So regardless of whether we think of literary appreciation in terms of sequential stages or porous categories, we need to look for tough texts that include characters with whom students are likely to relate. These characters should provide various entry points for readers to grow not only in their appreciation of literature but also in their lives.

Choices, Challenges, and Resolutions

As the quote from Reeves suggests, students want to read about characters who are wrestling with choices and challenges they themselves are facing. The following questions about choices and challenges are thus important in determining whether a book qualifies as a tough text:

- Do the characters wrestle with difficult social, emotional, and moral choices?

- Do these choices demand that the characters exercise values and, often, question those values?

- Do the challenges presented in the book show the great strength and resilience humans, especially adolescents, are capable of demonstrating?

- Does the ending of the book ring true? If the book ends on an ambiguous or down note, does it hold out the possibility of hope or justice, if not for the character then for the reader or the world?

In Pamela Hartman's study of working-class girls (2006), one participant, thinking about the choices Ophelia faces in *Hamlet*, says she "was kind of like playing detective basically":

> [Ophelia] was really confused. It was kind of what we're going through here in high school and everything. Like different problems, parents, siblings, and relationships—trying to figure out what you want and what you're happy with—just everything all jumbled together. And she's trying to figure it out, and it's kind of synonymous with what people are going through in high school really. . . . She's basically living what I'm trying to, kind of. (108)

A book club of girls in Beth's class also played detective as they read *Imani All Mine* (Porter 2000), drawing parallels between the challenges Tasha faces and those they or their friends had faced in real life. One of the most poignant moments occurred as they created their final project, a visual interpretation of what Tasha called a "Janus mask." (See Chapter 6 for a full description of this assignment and a depiction of the mask, in Figure 6.6.) The girls identified particularly with Tasha's poverty. When I asked Addy and Rachel why they had drawn dollar signs around Tasha's closed mouth, they explained that "even though Tasha was poor, she never talked about it" and neither did they. Addy explained that her experience of living in poverty was no more than an afterthought when she was a child: "Looking back, we had seven people living in a two-bedroom apartment, but I didn't realize we were poor at the time," she said. "I thought that was just the way it was." Rachel, on the other hand, said, "Man, I knew it when we were poor." She shook her head as she added, "Buttered noodles every night."

The characters in tough texts are so well drawn that students often find other points of connection in the larger social, emotional, and moral issues characters face. Even when they had not personally experienced circumstances similar to those the character had, Beth's, Cam's, and Rebecca's students often claimed they either knew someone who had or they could imagine the challenge as believable. In these cases, students applied the questions characters faced to their own lives or projected themselves into the characters' situations.

Cam's students saw connections between the choices the main character made in *Wringer* (Spinelli 2004) and the larger issue of violence, debating whether Palmer should defy the town's time-honored rite of passage that required ten-year-old boys to wring wounded birds' necks after a pigeon shoot. The students wrote this in their discussion record:

> One of the tough topics we talked about was violent behavior. The characters in our book dealt with this topic by avoiding it. Yes, we have [seen people outside school encounter violence], and they always go to a police officer or adult. Our book club discussed that violent behavior affects [people] emotionally and physically. We handled it like it's happened to us.

Even though Palmer's dilemma had no exact parallel in the students' personal lives, by projecting themselves into the story, these sixth graders were clearly able to wrestle with how they and others might respond to the violent behavior they saw in the world at large.

As I mentioned in the previous chapter, the difficult choices and challenges that characters in tough texts face aren't always neatly resolved by the end of the story. Even when these books end on an ambiguous or down note, however, they often demonstrate the great strength and resilience that humans, especially adolescents, can exercise in the face of challenges. They thus hold out the possibility that hope or justice will find a way, if not by the end of the book, then eventually. Tough texts are like the blues in this respect, honoring the tough reality of the moment by refusing to shy away from it while at the same time holding forth the hope that better times surely can't be too far away. I'm reminded of Laura Pritchett's comments to Beth's students about the ending of *Sky Bridge*, "Things can get better. But in real life, you have to fight for them to get better like Libby did."

Despite the promise of better days, the endings of tough texts can admittedly be hard to take. My daughter Lynley calls them "shoe-thrower endings," a reference to a time a romantic movie didn't turn out as we expected, making us both so frustrated we wanted to throw our shoes at the screen. All of us crave positive resolution in art because we hope for it in life. The best books, however, aren't morality plays. Kids sense this, too, and can spot an artificially optimistic ending faster than Holden Caulfield can spot a phony. Still, having taught or lived with adolescents all my adult life, I realize they can be emotionally, even acutely vulnerable at times. Knowing this, I've struggled throughout my career with whether it's okay to assign or recommend emotionally crushing texts like *Looking for Alaska* (Green 2005) or *The Chocolate War* (Cormier 1974) or to buy them for my own children. Should I protect my kids from literature that realistically deals with tragedy and injustice, or should I let literature break it to them gently and then make sure I'm there to support them through any emotional fallout? In contemplating these questions again while writing this book, I've returned to the moments in my own life when I've experienced tragedy via aesthetic experiences or firsthand.

When my husband and I took students on a tour of Europe several years ago, we visited the Museo de Arte Reina Sofia in Madrid, where Picasso's *Guernica* is housed. I'd never seen the painting before and knew nothing about the circumstances that inspired it, but as I stood before it in the museum, I knew how I was meant to respond. Everything about the painting—its massive size (11 feet by 25.6 feet), its literally bruising color scheme (black, white, and ashy grays), the textural immediacy conjured by Picasso's palpable brush strokes, and its figures (fractured buildings, felled bodies crying out, a menacing bull with a tail like a plume of smoke, ghostly heads, a woman holding a dying child)—meant to overwhelm.

Standing before the painting, my husband wiped his tears as he told me of the circumstances that inspired it. In 1937, during the Spanish Civil War, 1,600 people, most of them civilians, were killed or wounded when Generalissimo Franco allowed Hitler to conduct bombing practice over Guernica, a small village in northern Spain. The air attack lasted for over three hours; the village burned for three days. Picasso had been commissioned at the time to create a mural for the Spanish pavilion of the 1937 World's Fair, but was having difficulty finding an appropriate subject. After the bombing on Guernica, however, he created what has been called "modern art's most powerful antiwar statement" in a mere three months (Public Broadcasting System 1999).

As I listened to my husband relate the circumstances that inspired Picasso's masterpiece, my gut reaction to the painting began to make sense. We are not meant to find a hint of hope in the painting, just as we are not meant to view the circumstances it depicts as anything less than a holocaust. Instead, *Guernica* is meant to elicit the deepest, strongest, direst emotions that tragedy calls forth. My husband and I exited the museum bereft, stunned by atrocity even as we were awed by the art representing it. Neither of us could speak for a good while after we left, and even now the memory brings tears to my eyes. Yet I would not trade this aesthetic experience for blissful ignorance, because I believe it deepened my understanding of something elemental that I as a human being need to know.

This knowledge comes from the same deep well we all plumb when faced with a personal tragedy. As in art, so in life. While I was writing this book, two of my daughters' friends (one sixteen, the other seventeen) died, on separate occasions. On the evenings we learned of the deaths, there was no hope, nothing right to say, only a stunning, gaping loss. My daughters had grown up with these girls. Our families had forged the bonds you create only by standing together in the rain on the sidelines at soccer games or sitting in stuffy gymnasiums listening to a junior high choir sing. All of us who knew the families wanted desperately to do something, but there was nothing to be done that could bring these lovely girls back again, and that was what we wanted most of all. So in the end, we made soup and bread and sat with their parents and cried. Since then, the best we have been able to do is bear witness, to honor these bright lives together, with and in our grief. Empathy was our only choice.

Consequently, I no longer wrestle with whether it's permissible to assign age-appropriate books to adolescents that do not back away from atrocity and suffering; for as in life, so in literature. Knowing the story behind *Guernica* and watching my own adolescent children grapple with grief brought this truth to bear on my daily life. I grasped in a very real way what we as readers are supposed to understand about *Oedipus Rex* and *King Lear*—the unfortunate truth that tragedy, too, is an inevitable part of human existence.

In determining if a book is a tough text, we need to consider whether it raises very real and unsettling questions like those I and my family, and you and yours, have faced aesthetically and personally. When we look into the face of suffering, how are we to respond? With compassion? With contemplation? Is it enough to be moved without moving, or is a call to action implied? Once we are touched, are we also charged to transform and be transformed?

The choices, challenges, and endings of tough texts remind us both as readers and survivors that in facing these and other unsettling questions, empathy is often our only option. Our students may be wrestling with difficulties in their own lives like those of Tasha, Palmer, Libby, and other adolescent narrators, or they may just experience them through the safe distance that tough texts provide. Either way, I'm utterly certain that they need to see the great strength and resilience humans are capable of demonstrating in the face of apparently insurmountable challenges.

Student Appeal

Important questions to consider when gauging the student appeal of tough texts are:

- Is this a book my students would choose to read?

- Does this book cry out for conversation?

- Will my students see this as a book worth talking about with one another?

I've already touched on the first question by describing how students are drawn to books that include culturally relevant topics and relatable characters, so I'll focus on the last two questions here.

Because they are difficult by nature, tough texts are best read in the company of others. The books not only provoke substantive conversation but also benefit from the support provided by more emotionally mature readers, be they peers or teachers. Beth often recounts the story of an all-girls book club whose members were reading *The Perks of Being a Wallflower*. Knowing they would be discussing the scene in which Charlie's sister reveals that she has had an abortion, Beth positioned herself nearby, observing as she always does and taking notes in her teacher research journal. When she noticed one of the girls crying, she wrote, "Someone please hug Annie, someone please hug Annie!" And just as she was about to intervene, that's what happened. The girls comforted Annie and one another, bonding over the literature in a way that spilled over into their subsequent social interactions in the classroom.

Even when students think a book is appealing and find it worth discussing, they sometimes aren't able to process thorny passages as gracefully as this group did. In these cases, you may need to join the conversation briefly. Beth, Cam, Rebecca, and I have discovered that talking through difficult moments in tough texts invites students to bring up their own reactions. During these brief interchanges, students get the subtle but authentic chance to see how experienced readers engage emotionally with literature.

Literary Merit

Ask any group of students what they *choose* to read, and you'll soon discover that what award committees and teachers might consider pulp could very well be an adolescent's passion. We sometimes get hurt feelings when our students reject the favored texts that have made a significant impact on who we are as readers and human beings. Case in point: in reading "Self-Reliance" at the age of sixteen, I found a kindred spirit in Ralph Waldo Emerson. When both of my daughters read the essay at the same age, however, they begged to differ. "Transcendentalism—gag," one of them actually said, simulating the motion for full effect. I'm still not quite over the slight. On the other hand, they both burned through Stephenie Meyer's Twilight series, and they wouldn't let me rest until I'd read all the books too. I found them far less meaty but still entertaining, and now that my girls are a few years older, they've gotten over them, too.

Left to their own devices, many students aren't terribly adventurous when it comes to their reading, frequently opting for familiar titles and situations. I don't think this is much cause for alarm relative to their independent reading: it's their time, their choice. Be thankful they're reading and leave it at that. (Then, too, as Margaret Finders [1997] found in her study of the literacy habits of middle school girls, adolescents often tote around books their friends deem appropriate, but they don't always read them.)

The tables turn in class, however, when it's *our* time to read *together*. That doesn't mean that we should serve a steady diet of the texts we personally couldn't live without (e.g., "Self-Reliance"), but it also doesn't mean that we should choose texts that we suspect students will read on their own (e.g., *Twilight*). Our best bet is to look for books that will both engage and extend our students as readers, thus turning seemingly either/or options (either the kids will like it, and teachers will hate it or vice versa) into both/and possibilities (the kids will find it relevant, and teachers will find it worthwhile, too).

As you look for tough texts that meet the criteria I've reviewed so far, you'll also want to find books that you think are great, period. In other words, to merit classroom use, they should be of high literary merit. Keeping these questions in mind should help you:

- Is this book well crafted?

- Does style enhance content through the use of authentic adolescent voices, complex narrative structure, believable dialect, a variety of genres, or other stylistic features?

- Has the book earned external recognition, such as awards or outstanding reviews from reputable sources?

To navigate the slippery slope of what constitutes literary merit, we can take our cue from the criteria used for several book awards. To win the Newbery Medal, for instance, a book must be considered outstanding in the following categories:

- Interpretation of the theme or concept

- Presentation of information, to include accuracy, clarity, and organization

- Plot development

- Character delineation

- Setting delineation

- Appropriateness of style

Additional criteria considered for the Michael L. Printz Award, which honors YA literature, include voice, accuracy, and illustration. Selection committees for both awards are instructed to exclude didacticism or popularity in their consideration. In describing literary merit, the Printz Award committee goes so far as to say,

What is quality? We know what it is not. We hope the award will have a wide AUDIENCE among readers from 12 to 18 but POPULARITY is not the criterion for this award. Nor is MESSAGE. In accordance with the Library Bill of Rights, CONTROVERSY is not something to avoid. In fact, we want a book that readers will talk about.

Similarly, the Assembly on Literature for Adolescents of NCTE (ALAN) uses these criteria to determine the literary merit of the book selected for the Amelia Elizabeth Walden Award (AEWA), an honor bestowed annually on a work of fiction, preferably a novel, considered to be the year's most relevant title for young adults. AEWA award-winning books must:

- Contain well-developed characters

- Employ well-constructed forms suitable to function

- Include language and literary devices that enhance the narrative

- Suggest cogent and richly realized themes

- Present an authentic voice

When taken together, these lists of criteria suggest that the aesthetic features of well-told tales include fully developed characters facing authentic choices. The author's stylistic decisions, from word choice to a carefully crafted narrative structure, enhance the underlying themes of the text. The author provides insight into the human condition by believably depicting characters' fears and foibles, tears and triumphs, with sensitivity and compassion.

Resources for Locating Tough Texts

Where do you find books of the high literary merit that these awards criteria suggest? In my search for tough texts, I've been pleased to discover many resources that make my hunting happy. Besides the tried-and-true methods of browsing in the young adult section of bookstores and reading book reviews in the Sunday paper, I also rely on print and web resources that recommend books for adolescents. You'll find a list of these resources in Appendix A-2. The print resources include professional journals and books for teachers and librarians; the books may include booklists arranged by category and theme, annotations of books, tips for booktalks, and teaching rationales. The web resources direct you to lists of highly recommended and/or award-winning books and authors compiled by professional organizations, YA authors, and teens.

Justifying Your Use of Tough Texts

In the epigraph to this chapter, John Aikin, literary editor for the liberal *Monthly Magazine* in England from 1796–1807, quips that "an inquisitor's prohibited list" is the place to find good books (1796, 179).

Because tough texts are by nature controversial, it's possible that parents, administrators, and even some students might object if you assign them in your classroom. During the many years I taught secondary English and now that I spend considerable time partnering with schools, parents have challenged books (both tough texts) on only two occasions. In one instance, a parent objected to the graphic content of *The Bell Jar* (Plath 1963), which her daughter had selected as part of an independent study in my eleventh-grade English class. In the other, parents objected to the language in *The Curious Incident of the Dog in the Nighttime* (Haddon 2003), which their son had selected to read in a book club in Rebecca's pre-AP literature class. Violence, religion, profanity, and sexual content are the most common reasons books are challenged, according to the National Coalition Against Censorship (NCAC). In the end, both instances were positively resolved for two simple but powerful reasons— choice and preparation.

Provide Choices

The NCTE's "Guideline on the Students' Right to Read" (1981) argues: "The right of any individual not just to read but to read whatever he or she wants to read is basic to a democratic society." At the same time, however, the NCTE acknowledges that this right,

> like all rights guaranteed or implied within our constitutional tradition, can be used wisely or foolishly. In many ways, education is an effort to improve the quality of choices open to all students. But to deny the freedom of choice in fear that it may be unwisely used is to destroy the freedom itself. For this reason, we respect the right of individuals to be selective in their own reading.

In her provocative article "A Battle Reconsidered: Second Thoughts on Book Censorship and Conservative Parents," Suzanne Kauer notes that many teachers, she among them, cast the challenges they face in teaching controversial texts in militant terms, speaking of "'arming' themselves to 'battle' with parents" (2008, 60). Yet as "The Right to Read" points out, we must respect individuals' rights—and I would add parents' rights—to select what they and their children will read.

Providing choices among tough texts is the best way I know to do so and forestall objections to those books at the same time. While you will undoubtedly want to teach tough texts to a whole class on occasion, I highly recommend whenever possible using a number of texts at once in a small-group or book club setting. Providing choice from a range of books that might be related by theme or by mere virtue of their being tough texts gives your students the opportunity to practice civil discourse.

The concept of green-light and yellow-light books, which I describe in *The Book Club Companion* (2006), can come in handy as you make your choices. In brief, *green-light texts* are so frequently taught in schools that even though they focus on culturally significant and often controversial issues, they are unlikely to raise objections. These books often appeal to more conservative students and their parents because they have an unofficial seal of approval that gives them a level of familiarity, status, and thus safety. The mother of a girl on my daughter's soccer team said she had no qualms about the books her child would be reading in English that year because they were the "best books" to read and teach. While I agreed that there were some awfully good books on the list, what made them green-light books in her eyes was that they were the same ones she had read in high school. *Cry, the Beloved Country* (Paton 1948) is a good example of a green-light tough text, because it enjoys the "classic" label while still dealing with the sticky topic of race relations.

Even though the topics and issues in green-light books may be just as controversial as those included in *yellow-light* books, the latter are likely to be more explicit in content and language. These books have often been more recently published as well, which means both that parents are less likely to be familiar with the titles and that the language is often more easily understood. *The Giver* (Lowry 1993) is a good example of a yellow-light book; despite its controversial content (e.g., infanticide, euthanasia, sexual references), it is written at about a fifth-grade reading level.

What keeps these books from veering into red-light territory is that you still consider them to be emotionally appropriate and intellectually beneficial for students in a given class in your particular school and community to read. Admittedly, "appropriateness" can be difficult to determine, because it often lies in the eyes of the beholder. If you are new to a school, asking a trusted colleague's opinion about a book can help you determine its appropriateness. While you probably have a good idea about your students' maturity level, it's also key to keep community sensibilities in mind.

If you've taught in more than one place, you know that your book lists are likely to vary from school to school. For example, I was able to use *The Color Purple* (Walker 1982) in book clubs in an eleventh-grade honors English class in a university town, but I wouldn't have tried it in the regular track, tenth-grade class in the more conservative school I'd taught in before. Same state, same-sized school, but grade level, academic track (for some reason, advanced students are judged to be more mature), and prevailing community values made the difference. Achieving tenure didn't hurt either. This can be true even within the same district. While *The Perks of Being a Wallflower* (Chbosky 1999) was an appropriate choice for Beth's students at an alternative high school where guidelines were more relaxed, Rebecca said that she most likely would not be able to teach the book at her more conservative suburban high school on the other side of the same city.

My point is that you have to weigh the headaches you stand to endure when you assign any book against the benefits you think your students will gain by reading it. One could argue that my not assigning *The Color Purple* deprived my tenth graders of the opportunity to read a terrific book. My response is that there are books you teach to a whole class, those you make available to small groups, and others you recommend to individual students. These generally aren't the same books. Judging when to do what with which book is a matter of professional judgment based in part on respect for those you teach and their caregivers.

Thinking about books with families you know in mind can be a good reality check. Would this be an appropriate book for your same-age child, niece, or nephew to read? Would the family of that child be likely to agree? The latter question is crucial. The books I recommend for my nephew Jayce vary from those I suggest to my son, Austen, even though the boys are the same age, because my views are generally more liberal than my sister's. Imagining a class in which both Jayce and Austen are students helps me think about the range of books I'll make available.

Once you have decided which tough texts you want to assign, you need to be up front with both students and their parents about what they entail. If you decide to offer several books in a book club or small-group context, being frank with students about content and language during booktalks will allow them to determine whether they (or their parents) will feel comfortable reading and discussing a book with their peers. ReLeah Cossett Lent points out that "when students take responsibility for their reading within the boundaries of their family's standards, the burden shifts to the reader—where it rightly belongs" (2008, 62). If you also give students a chance to preview the books in class before stating their preference, you don't have to go into great detail in your booktalks. When Rebecca introduces *Postcards from No Man's Land* (Chambers 1999), for instance, she describes the plot and simply explains that the protagonist confronts issues of sexuality and euthanasia. Students who don't feel comfortable discussing these subjects choose other books.

The beauty of giving book clubs several great books from which to choose is that students won't have a diminished experience just because they've opted out of a particular book. Furthermore, they'll have the benefit of hearing about the books they haven't read when peers from other book clubs share their responses in whole-class activities and final projects. As Rebecca, Cam, and Beth have discovered, students often voluntarily go on to read books their peers from other book clubs have recommended. Perhaps the extended preview the civil discourse sequence provides, combined with the opportunity to read a text individually that they might not feel ready to discuss publicly, makes them feel comfortable doing so.

Different options exist for informing parents about the tough texts you plan to teach. While sending *permission slips* home for each book might be the most obvious, I don't recommend this route unless your school requires it. Doing so for every tough text is an impractical amount of work for you and could very well wind up being counterproductive by raising parents' suspicions unnecessarily. When I taught at the secondary level, I had more success with a *syllabus review*. At the beginning of the year, I sent home a course syllabus that listed the books students would be asked to read in my class. In a brief cover letter, I asked parents or guardians to review the syllabus and return it with their signature to indicate that they had reviewed the content of the course, including the titles their child would be asked to read. (These days I'd also suggest that parents consult online resources like amazon.com or powells.com where they could read summaries and brief reviews for the books.) I also encouraged them to contact me if they had concerns and assured them that I respected their wishes and concerns regarding their child's education. I provided a box on the signature page that they could check if they had questions and a place where they could list contact information so that I could follow up. As a way of increasing the chances that the signatures would be returned, I explained that students would receive a participation grade for returning the signed syllabus to me. Another option some teachers prefer is the *non-permission slip*, which parents sign and return only if they object to the curriculum at hand.

However you inform students and parents, remember that choice equals power. "What are parents really asking for when they say no to a book? How can we accommodate reasonable requests without compromising our curriculum?" (Kauer 2008, 60). In the cases I mentioned above with *The Bell Jar* and *The Curious Incident of the Dog in the Nighttime*, both Rebecca and I were able to keep parents as allies, not enemies, because we made other options available so that their children could successfully complete the assignment. I varied the requirements of the independent study slightly so that my student could consult biographical sources on Sylvia Plath instead of reading *The Bell Jar*, and Rebecca simply explained that *The Curious Incident* was one among several choices her student could read. Providing these choices went a long way toward earning respect, because we held true to the principle that both students and parents have rights concerning what they read.

Create a Rationale

As a former basketball coach, I know that the best offense is a good defense. This principle is relevant for justifying your use of tough texts as well, especially since many of the titles I've mentioned show up on lists of challenged and banned books. (To distinguish these terms, *challenged* books are exactly that; someone, often a parent, challenges whether a book should be allowed in a classroom or a library. *Banned* books, on the other hand, have been removed from the shelves so that no one has access to them.) As a principal's wife, I know that administrators typically become aware of the books you're teaching only if a parent calls to complain. Before this happens, you should be able to articulate why out of all the books you might teach, this one is worth the trouble. Based on her encounter with a thoughtful parent who respectfully challenged virtually every book in her curriculum, Suzanne Kauer reports that the question "How do I justify these works?" shifted to "Why do we choose what we do in English classrooms?" (2008, 58). Answering either question requires that you have a rationale.

At the Anti-Censorship Center on the NCTE website, you can find a Starter Sheet called "How to Write a Rationale." This document acknowledges as unrealistic the expectation that teachers will write detailed rationales for every book they teach and instead suggests thinking about rationales on four levels of formality. At the lowest level is a brief written statement articulating why and how a book fits into your curriculum. The next level of formality involves completing any simple forms your department or school might require. If you wish to propose that a book be approved to teach in a particular class, you probably would need to move on to the third level, fully developing a written rationale according to your district's process for getting texts added to the list of those approved to teach. At the final level of formality are published rationales of frequently challenged books.

In circumstances where a detailed written rationale is required, the Starter Sheet suggests the following categories and provides detailed guidelines for addressing them:

- Bibliographic citation

- Intended audience of students (class and/or grade level)

- Brief summary of the work

- Relationship of the work to the program (e.g., course objectives, methods of teaching and assessment)

- Potential impact of the work on students

- Potential problems with the work

- Other information about the work (e.g., book reviews, booklists, awards)

- Other supplementary materials (e.g, author biography)

- A list of rationales for using the work that have been published by other educators

- Alternative selections an individual student might read if parents objected to the work

The website also provides sample rationales. These include additional elements such as a description of literary qualities, theoretical support, a summary of reviews, and a discussion of why the book should not be banned.

Appendix A-3 lists several books, journals, and websites to help you prepare in advance for challenges to tough texts you want to teach. In the event of a challenge, it's difficult *not* to resort to martial metaphors; challenges to your curriculum feel like challenges to your professional judgment because they are. But being equipped with a rationale increases the chances that parents—and your administrator, for that matter—will view your judgment as sound. In the event of a challenge, listen to and respect all parties involved, articulate your rationale, and work together to reach a mutually agreeable solution.

In selecting tough texts for your classroom, maintaining a balance between the questions I suggest in the heuristic described earlier as well as the questions of appropriateness I suggest above should help you determine which books should make the cut. While the sum of the whole is what really matters, working through these questions individually should help you determine which texts will ultimately work best for you, parents, the school, and ultimately for your students, the most important readers of all.

Chapter 4

Curiously enough, the linguistic skill that seems to develop earliest, the one in which we all engage most often and with most enthusiasm, the one we don't resist with all the stubbornness at our command, the one that seems most natural is also, apparently, the skill that we have neglected most seriously in the schools. And that's talk.

—ROBERT PROBST

My husband and I never thought our daughter Lexie would learn to crawl. My library of parenting manuals said crawling was an important developmental milestone, so we were worried. Our pediatrician rolled his eyes, and of course he was right. She crawled for approximately five minutes before showing signs that she was ready to walk, but our parental anxiety over the crawling thing probably accounts for my husband's determination to teach her. He would stand behind her, place her feet on top of his, and slo-o-o-o-wly move forward one foot at a time. Soon she was brave enough to take a tentative first step on her own, and life as we knew it was over; she was into everything. Learning to talk was a different story. Lexie needed absolutely no assistance with *that* developmental milestone (and still doesn't to this day!).

Setting Up for Civil Discourse

Because verbal communication comes as naturally to our students as it did to Lexie, we perhaps assume they don't need much help with it in school. When talking about tough texts, however, they do. It's essential that we provide *perpetual scaffolding* through an array of procedures and strategies to ease students into civil discourse so they can eventually carry it out on their own.

The Notion of Perpetual Scaffolding

You're probably already familiar with the concept of scaffolding (Bruner 1975)—the need for teachers to provide more support early on when students are learning a new skill or strategy before gradually withdrawing that support as they proceed (see also Vygotsky 1978). Lots of early support is helpful for many processes, as my daughter's experiences with becoming ambulatory suggest. Although my husband probably didn't officially teach her to walk, he did provide just enough help to facilitate forward movement before she took off on her own.

When learning to engage in civil discourse, students need variable yet persistent support from start to finish in a civil discourse sequence (CDS). For one thing, even though the contemporary language in most tough texts is easy to decode, their structural or stylistic complexity, as well as the "bigness" of the culturally significant questions, will almost certainly present intellectual challenges. When students grumble, "Why is this book so hard?" we need to know that they aren't just talking about decoding words or discerning basic plot details.[1] Drawing on Steiner (1978), who poses the question behind this question, I believe that when students complain, they may be having these types of difficulty:

1. Contingent difficulty: *What does this text (or this word or reference in the text) mean?*

2. Modal difficulty: *What kind of text is this?*

3. Tactical difficulty: *Why is the author doing this? What is the point of this technique?*

4. Ontological difficulty: *Where is the author coming from?*

(See Figure 4.1.)

As Steiner points out, only ontological difficulty is ultimately insurmountable, but even this challenge can be useful in helping readers grow and develop empathy. Students need perpetual scaffolding when they encounter any of these kinds of difficulty, at least until they are confident enough as readers to tackle the challenges tough texts present as a matter of course.

A second reason perpetual scaffolding is so important is that students also need help with tough talk. Because students so rarely see enactments of civil discourse in our culture, schools are charged with taking up the task (Probst 2007). You may be thinking, "Oh, great, yet another to-do item on my already long list that includes bully-proofing, character education, leaving no child behind,

---

[1] If this is the case, however, Kylene Beers' book *When Kids Can't Read—What Teachers Can Do* (2002) is an invaluable resource for helping students unlock basic meaning.

Tough Talk, Tough Texts

Figure 4.1 - Four kinds of difficulty in understanding what we read

Kind of Difficulty	When It Occurs	Examples	Solution
Contingent			
Elicits the question, "What does this mean?"	Occurs when the reader does not understand the definition of a word or phrase, an idiom or allusion, or the significance of a cultural reference the author is using.	Denotative meanings of words Biblical or mythological allusions Shakespeare's frequent use of double entendre in *Romeo and Juliet*	Look it up: "In the overwhelming majority of cases, what we mean by saying 'this is difficult' signifies 'this is a word, a phrase or a reference which I will have to look up'" (Steiner 1978, 27).
Modal			
Elicits the question, "What kind of text is this?"	Occurs when the reader is unfamiliar with the way the piece is constructed (i.e., the form or genre of the text). The text feels in some way "unnatural," and the reader doesn't fully apprehend or like it as a result.	Epistolary novel (e.g, *The Perks of Being a Wallflower*) Dystopian novel (e.g., *The Giver, Feed*) Multiple story lines (e.g., *Postcards from No Man's Land*)	Trust the text. Read with an open mind in an attempt to accustom oneself to the mode.
Tactical			
Elicits the questions, "Why is the author doing this? What's the point of this technique?"	Occurs when the reader doesn't understand how or why the author is attempting to shape her/his reading of the text in a particular way.	Deliberate withholding of information (e.g., *The Adventures of Sherlock Holmes*) Unreliable narrator (e.g., *The Catcher in the Rye*) Use of multiple narrators or story lines (e.g., *In the Time of the Butterflies*) Ambiguous ending (e.g., *Life of Pi*)	Trust the author, assuming that she or he is telling the story in a certain way so that it will have a particular effect. Be patient with yourself, knowing that "we are not meant to understand easily and quickly. . . . The text [will yield] its force and singularity of being only gradually" (Steiner 1978, 35).
Ontological			
Elicits the question, "Where is the author coming from?"	Occurs when the reader has difficulty understanding the "map of meaning" (Steiner 1978, 45) implicit in the text, that is, the worldview the author or text is conveying.	Clash between Chicano myth and traditional Catholicism (e.g., *Bless Me, Ultima*) Transposition of traditional system of good and evil (e.g., *The Golden Compass*)	Realize that this difficulty is ultimately insurmountable. You can only work toward this kind of understanding, which requires expanding your vision to encompass alternative worldviews. In short, you as a reader must change. *But* the pay-off of your attempt is that *you get to grow.*

Adapted from G. Steiner, *On Difficulty and Other Essays*, New York: Oxford University Press (1978).

teaching them to just say no, and equipping them with twenty-first-century literacy skills." But think about how the muscles in your neck tense or your palms get sweaty in everyday conversation when someone sings the praises of the political candidate you can't abide. Consider the temptation you feel when someone—a friend, let's say, to up the ante—asks you to weigh in on a difficult social issue, especially one on which you suspect the two of you won't see eye-to-eye.

If we, as mature, mostly level-headed educators, feel the fight-or-flight urge, it should be clear that it will take more than frontloading to help our students engage in honest, open discussion about the issues that are common to tough texts. Probst says it's important to teach tough talk because

> at least some of the conversations our students will undertake in the future may shape the society in which we all will live. If they are to participate in those conversations effectively, productively, and for the common good, they have to develop the predispositions, the habits, and the standards that will make such participation possible. (2007, 45–46)

You'll provide three types of scaffolding throughout a CDS to help kids with textual difficulties and the challenges of tough talk: (1) exoscaffolding, (2) endoscaffolding, and (3) metatalk.

From junior high science you may remember the difference between the exoskeleton of an insect (the hard outer shell) and the endoskeleton (the internal "squishy" parts). You can think about perpetual scaffolding in similar terms.

Exoscaffolding refers to the "shell" or frame that teachers set up for the entire class so that students can understand the notion of civil discourse and learn strategies for carrying it out in small-group and whole-class discussions. Exoscaffolding is the teacher-*directed* work that takes place *outside* student-led discussions.

Endoscaffolding refers to the occasional drop-in visits teachers make during small-group discussions to answer quick questions about contingent difficulties in texts, restart stalled discussions, or nudge students through an impasse. Endoscaffolding is the teacher-*facilitated* process that takes place *within* small groups and is tailored to the particular needs of the moment.

Metatalk is the "talk about talk" that makes students aware of the dispositions and strategies they're practicing so that they can use them again in contexts outside the classroom. Metatalk helps students reflect on their use of civil discourse throughout a CDS.

In a nutshell, then, exoscaffolding provides a *framework*, endoscaffolding offers *intervention*, and metatalk enables *reflection*. Although in the rest of the book these terms will be used in connection with strategies that may be necessary at particular moments, the remainder of this chapter focuses on tools for exoscaffolding.

The degree of exoscaffolding you'll need to provide varies; it's doubtful you'll use all of the tools described below in any given CDS. How to pick and choose? If all the practices are useful, which ones are best? The short answer: it depends. The long answer: there are no guarantees that what "worked" with the sleepy kids in first period will work with the antsy kids right before lunch or the hyper ones in the period immediately after. The longer you teach, the more adept you become at finessing your teaching approach depending on the demographics, the particular mix of kids in your classroom, the time of day and year, and a score of other variables—in other words, the more aware you become that context is key to authentic teaching and learning.

We forget this at our peril. If you and your students have felt frustrated by what I call the "fallout curricula" that has spun out of No Child Left Behind (NCLB) over the years—all those boxes and kits and binders of what (supposedly) works—you know exactly what I mean. No matter how well-meaning, no script in any teacher's guide is sufficient preparation for meeting all students' needs. And none of them are worth a nickel compared with the thoughtful and committed teacher who is able to choose from a host of consistently reliable, as opposed to uniformly "best," practices according to his or her teaching context.

Nor is there is a single perfect combination of tools or algorithm to follow in using them. Like Beth, Cam, and Rebecca, you should pick and choose those that meet the needs of your students. This isn't a disclaimer; it's a reality that applies both to teaching students to engage in civil discourse and, more generally, to teaching in general. We do well to embrace it, because it keeps us learning as we teach and rescues us from the clutches of boredom.

Norming Methods: Scenarios, Debriefing Discussions, Quickwrites, and Starter Texts

As Rebecca and I learned from experience, defining civil discourse is an important first step in helping students learn how to practice it. Students need to know the cultural significance of what you're asking them to do and why you believe they're capable of doing it both in and outside your classroom. If a common definition for civil discourse existed, we might proceed straightforwardly, defining the term, explaining our expectations for our students' behavior, and providing some helpful guidelines for discussing the controversial issues that crop up in tough texts. But even if we were able to do so, I'm not sure this deductive approach would ensure that everyone is on the same page. Norms for participation that are authentic and thus workable cannot be imposed. Instead, they must be articulated and regulated by group members themselves because successful norming always requires buy-in. The following methods should help you achieve it.

Scenarios and Debriefing Discussions

Articulating norms is by definition pretty abstract even for adults, often resulting in nebulous admonitions like "show respect." Scenarios are an inductive method for helping students name the concrete behavior they wish to foster or avoid in the name of enacting civil discourse. The What Is *Civil Discourse?* handout in Chapter 1 (Figure 1.1) lists scenarios that have occurred in actual book clubs while students are discussing tough texts. By discussing these scenarios, students come up with their own workable solutions to the inevitable problems that arise when talking about tough texts. What will they do if a group member quashes dissent by holding forth on her opinion? How will they react if someone disagrees with their interpretation of a scene or challenges their worldview on a controversial issue?

Asking small groups to arrive at potential solutions *before* these scenarios take place paves the way for another essential part of the norming process—the debriefing discussion. Debriefing discussions are whole-class conversations that you facilitate to help students crystallize the ideas that have emerged in the course of an activity. They can be useful throughout the CDS, but when used in conjunction with the scenarios exercise, they serve a three-fold purpose:

1. Sharing the solutions that groups have generated in regard to scenarios so that all students can benefit from ideas their group didn't think of

2. Establishing a class list of norms to guide teacher-facilitated discussion of some introductory whole-class texts

3. Extrapolating an initial definition of civil discourse

The class list of norms is also a helpful reference when students later divide into small groups to generate their own norms for discussing tough texts independently.

In our experiences with high school students, Beth, Rebecca, and I learned the hard way that debriefing discussions are an essential part of the exoscaffolding you need to use with the scenarios exercise and elsewhere in the CDS. Without a debriefing discussion, Rebecca's pre-AP tenth graders approached the scenarios as "another day, another worksheet." And even though Beth's students receive special training in communication skills before they are allowed to attend regular classes at the alternative high school, "their skills went right out the window" (Beth's words) the day we introduced scenarios. Some groups generated solutions that were so vague as to be meaningless ("have civil discourse," for example), and one group's every suggestion was dripping with sarcasm (my favorite was "act like gladiators").

Although we initially wondered if we should scrap the scenarios altogether with subsequent classes, we still sensed their potential. We made a few simple adjustments, such as asking students to write down the highlights of their small-group discussion and report to the rest of the class and then articulating some whole-class norms in a debriefing discussion. Recording the highlights of their small-group discussion helped students stay on task, added a degree of seriousness to their work, and helped focus the debriefing session that followed. During that debriefing, students pooled their brainpower to come up with solutions to some common problems that can arise during controversial discussions. In both classrooms, Beth's and Rebecca's skillful facilitation during whole-class debriefings also helped students become more conscious of the significance of what they were accomplishing by engaging in civil discourse. (For a reminder of the procedures they followed, see Chapter 1.)

Quickwrites

Douglas Barnes (1992) describes the potential of "exploratory talk" for stretching thinking, wrestling with challenging ideas, and taking the risk to grow. Barnes's definition can easily be extended to writing, particularly to the quickwrite[2]—a brief piece of exploratory writing intended to help students rehearse their ideas on a topic or question before sharing them in discussion. Later in this chapter I'll talk about how quickwrites function in other stages of a CDS as well. Here I want to focus on how quickwrites can give students who need a bit more social

[2]I use *quickwrite* as a synonym for *freewrite* because this is the term Beth, Cam, and Rebecca use with their students. Some educators consider quickwrites to be much shorter, as brief as a minute, so think "freewrite" if you find this substitution troublesome.

support or buy-in the extra time they need to spend with specific aspects of norming. As part of the norming process, quickwrites can help students explore definitions of commonly used terms related to civil discourse, brainstorm solutions to problems that might arise in discussion, and describe the steps they as individuals will take to engage in civil discourse.

Quickwrites are exactly what the term says. Students write briefly without stopping (five to ten minutes, depending on the age and fluency of the student) in response to a written prompt you provide on the board, in a handout, or online. If you regularly use print or digital journals in class (blogs, discussion forums, and so on), your students already have a great space in which to store quickwrites. If journals aren't already part of your classroom routine, I strongly recommend using them temporarily during a CDS. Here are some sample quickwrite prompts Beth, Cam, and Rebecca have used during the norming process:

- What is controversy? What are some topics that you consider controversial? Why?

- Choose three of the scenarios listed on the What Is *Civil Discourse?* handout and write about how you would handle a similar situation. What would *you* do? What should *your group* do?

- Choose two or three of the solutions our class listed in response to the scenarios and describe how they might play out. What does it mean to "show respect," "speak for yourself," "listen well," and so on? What does it sound like, look like, feel like on the inside?

- If you are watching a group discuss a controversial topic, how do you know whether someone is participating in civil discourse? What will he be doing? How will she be acting and reacting? Think about body language, gestures, and tone of voice.

- We've been talking about what it means to have "an elephant in the room"—a controversial topic that everyone ignores. What will you do if an "elephant" enters the room while you are discussing your book?

Used in conjunction with debriefing discussions, quickwriting to prompts like these allows students to develop finer-grained plans than they might by using the scenarios activity by itself.

Here I want to acknowledge a teacherly elephant in the room because I suspect it will resonate with you. As much as I love using quickwrites to focus students' attention on prompts like these, I've had a love-hate relationship with journals over the years. On one hand, they are efficient, convenient, and nonnegotiable. For the student who struggles with keeping track of papers, never mind organizing them, journals keep quickwrites in one place. Although I now use digital journals almost exclusively, I used to store print journals in boxes, labeled by class period, that stayed in my classroom. (I liked those marbled composition notebooks with the sturdy covers, because they were inexpensive yet held up well.) Because writing in a journal (whether on paper or digitally) is an in-class activity, it has a "no-excuses" appeal. Journals don't get stored in lockers, they don't go home for homework, so no one has an excuse for not writing. When students see journal writing listed on the daily agenda as they enter the classroom, they quickly learn the routine of grabbing their bound journals from the class box or logging on to their e-journal and responding at the proper time to the prompt you've provided.

On the other hand, journals have their disadvantages. Bound journals are heavy, and I hate, hate, hate lugging boxes of them home to read. If you still prefer hard copies but share the (often quite literal) pain of carrying around boxes of bound journals, you may want to use blue books—those thin, 7-by-8½-inch booklets college students use for in-class exams—as dedicated journals for a CDS. I can buy blue books at the university bookstore for twenty-five cents apiece, but they are also available online at various office supplies websites for around thirty cents. At sixteen pages, blue books are lengthy enough to accommodate several quickwrites during a specific CDS, but thin enough to store in file folders or to hole-punch for loose-leaf binders if you want to collect quickwrites from several units throughout the year.

Another thing I love about journals is seeing how kids have wrestled with their thinking. Yet like almost every English teacher I know, I've struggled over the years with managing the paperload, and I commiserate regularly with my friend and colleague Louann Reid. She says that students need far more practice writing than any English teacher can possibly read, but we both agree that as much as students need teachers who require writing on a regular basis, they also need teachers who have lives outside school and we need to give ourselves a break.

When I suggest this to my college students who are studying to be teachers, they look at me aghast. You may have the same response. But humor me for a moment and do the math. My college students reason that if a student spends five minutes writing a journal entry, a teacher should spend at least that much time responding. Assuming a teacher has an average of 150 students—a not unreasonable estimate given today's large class sizes—here's how the numbers play out:

150 students
$\times$ 5 minutes to read and respond per journal entry
$\times$ 3 entries per week
= 2,250 minutes = 37.5 hours *on journals alone* per week (about 7.5 hours a day, 5 days a week, or the close equivalent of a full-time job!)

My college students are aghast, and no matter how many times I perform this little exercise, so am I. It always leads me to the same conclusion, however: shouldering such a task is ridiculously impossible. I'm not suggesting that we abandon our responsibility to read and respond to our students' writing, but we do have to be realistic about managing the paperload, or we will resent ourselves right out of our jobs.

Here's what that means regarding responding to quickwrites. Because these are always "first-draft finals," to borrow a term from Nancie Atwell (2007), we can read and evaluate them accordingly. When you're writing your way into new ideas, do you want anyone to evaluate your first thoughts as if they were your best thoughts? I think not. Well, neither do your students. Reminding yourself and being up front with your students about that can help you both establish realistic expectations for response.

I explain to my students that I do "quickreads" of quickwrites, giving checkmarks for content and completion only, not for conventions, though I ask that they write as correctly as they can. They get full credit for writing thoughtfully to the prompt for the entire time. I also employ selective reading, meaning I don't read and respond to every entry (my goal is about one out of every six entries depending on my total number of students); sometimes I allow them to star entries to guide my selective reading, and sometimes I choose entries randomly. I like William Stafford's approach to responding: "My job [is] not to correct but understand and participate. A student's paper [is] a test for me. . . . My remarks [are] meant to show my accompaniment, sometimes my readiness to learn more" (1986, 18). When I do respond to quickwrites, my goal, like Stafford's, is to make brief "readerly" comments as opposed to evaluative ones. I describe how an entry pushed my thinking or pose a question to push students' thinking rather than commenting on how they should improve their writing, which is a task I reserve for more polished drafts.

I also explain to students that I won't be their sole audience. When the purpose of a quickwrite is to prompt discussion, for instance, I'll sometimes ask them to read back over what they've written and highlight or underline their best line. Then we'll do a quick read-around and begin our discussion based on these ideas. Other times I'll ask them to pair-share aloud with a classmate or to exchange quickwrites and write a brief response, friendly-letter style.

And I'll occasionally ask them to write for themselves, browsing through a few of their previous quickwrites and writing a summative reflection about the most interesting ideas they've found and how their thinking has developed since they wrote them. I make it clear that when they've shared with their classmate(s) or responded to themselves, I won't comment on those entries. I also promise to let them know *before* they begin writing if they will be sharing it with classmates afterward so they can adjust the degree of intimate detail they want to reveal.

While these suggestions don't completely eliminate the burden of responding to quickwrites, they lessen it significantly by limiting the number of pages read and dividing the labor that remains. Doing the math again:

150 students

× 5 minutes to read and respond to one journal entry

× 1 of every 6 entries (about 1 every two weeks)

= 750 minutes = 12.5 hours on journals every two weeks (a little over an hour a day, 5 days a week)

If this total still discourages you, remember it assumes students are doing quickwrites at the rate of four every two weeks. Since quickwrites are a tool you'll use sparingly, this almost certainly won't be your grading pace for the entire CDS. Nevertheless, as a go-to tool you can use throughout a CDS, I think you'll find quickwrites worth the time. William Faulkner once remarked, "I never know what I think about something until I read what I've written on it." Following Faulkner's lead, students can gain the confidence and clarity they need to share their thoughts with others by rehearsing their thoughts in quickwrites.

Starter Texts

Once you're satisfied that students have developed a solid set of norms they can use to negotiate difficult topics, you're ready for the next important piece of exoscaffolding—using starter texts to introduce them to the response strategies they'll use throughout a CDS. Because learning to talk about tough texts is so complex, you'll want to pace students' way through the process. Introducing new strategies gradually and providing enough time to practice them on briefer tough texts, or "starter texts" as I call them, allows you to gradually withdraw your support once you sense that students are ready to go it alone.

As the term implies, starter texts are used at the beginning of a CDS. Most often, starter texts favor brief genres—think song lyrics, poetry, and short stories—presented in order of textual difficulty and level of controversy. With her pre-AP tenth graders one semester, Rebecca used a relatively noncontroversial short story, followed by a more contemporary short story focused on racism yet written in accessible language, followed by a more textually challenging long poem on the Holocaust. As you select texts, also think about thematic connections; in this case, all three texts Rebecca used were focused on "defining moments," a theme related to the books students read next.

There is no magic formula for assembling a set of starter texts. Because some students need more scaffolding than others, the length and number of starter texts you'll use and the amount of time you allot to them will vary according to the intellectual and emotional readiness of a particular class—a level only you can gauge and one that will change from class to class and year to year. As a general rule, however, the following sequence works well if you plan to use three or more starter texts:

1. Whole-class discussion of *challenging* starter text(s)

2. Small-group discussion of *more accessible* starter text(s)

3. Small-group discussion of *more challenging* starter text(s)

4. Small-group discussion of a *book-length challenging text*

If you plan to use fewer starter texts, the underlying principle should still be moving from whole-class to small-group discussion. This structure gradually eases students into the independent discussion of tough texts by allowing you to provide optimal up-front support.

While most starter texts in a CDS are "mini" tough texts, younger students may first need to apply the cognitive skills that the response strategies require to less controversial texts. Once they're comfortable using the response strategies in small groups, they can then add the emotional load tough texts require. One year when student ability dictated and time allowed, Cameron first grouped his students into book clubs to read lighter novels (e.g., *Gifts, Hatchet,*

Walk Two Moons) before regrouping them in civil discourse book clubs to read tough texts like *The Giver* and *Wringer*. In other years, an intensive examination of song lyrics has been sufficient preparation for book club discussions of tough texts. Cameron has used John Mayer's "Waiting on the World to Change" as a starter text because the lyrics are accessible and thematically relevant to considering the connection between civil discourse and social justice.

Regardless of the number of starter texts you use, remember that your overall objective is "handover" (Bomer 2007)—that is, gradually shifting the responsibility for engaging in civil discourse to students. Here are some questions to keep in mind as you select and order your starter texts:

- How many starter texts is this group of students likely to need? (Pad this number a bit so you'll be prepared if students need more practice than you anticipated.)

- Are there certain genres students will encounter independently later in the CDS? If so, what are some accessible examples of these genres that you could use as starter texts?

- Do you want to select texts with thematic connections or not?

- Which texts are most textually accessible? Which are more difficult?

- Which texts are less controversial? Which are more so?

- Do the above factors suggest a sequence that will gradually ease students into an independent discussion of tough texts?

The length of starter texts may also be a consideration, depending on whether the entire CDS will focus on a collection of shorter texts or, more commonly, will include a small number of starter texts leading to a book-length text. Finally, certain texts may pair more naturally with some response strategies. As you'll see in the next section, just as starter texts are carefully ordered, so too are the strategies and the contexts you'll use to introduce them.

Introduction to Sticky Notes, Bookmarks, and Dailies

Over the years, Beth, Cam, Rebecca, and I have experimented with a number of response strategies. When working with tough texts, we keep returning to three—sticky notes, bookmarks, and dailies. I'll describe sticky notes at length since they are the foundation for the other two, then provide thumbnail descriptions of bookmarks and dailies, which mostly come into play in connection with the book-length texts students read later in the CDS.

Chapter 5 offers further examples of how these three strategies are used in combination. Think layering: sticky notes with the first starter text, followed by sticky notes plus the bookmark with the next text, and finally the trio of sticky notes, the bookmark, and dailies with subsequent texts. Each strategy builds on the prior one, easing students into talking about tough texts independently. Introducing them in sequence gives you ample time to model using the strategies to participate in controversial discussions, monitor how much instructional support students need, and adjust the pace as necessary.

Sticky Notes

While some teachers are in favor of spending textbook budgets on sticky notes and trade books (Beers 2002), others object that an authentic reading experience can get lost in a blizzard of sticky notes (Gallagher 2009). I should probably own stock in 3M. I ask students to use sticky notes for the same reasons I use them in my own reading: they are in-text notes to myself in which I mark lines and passages that strike me as important in some way so that I can return to them later for further consideration either privately or with other readers, like members of my own book club.

Because I could fill up every margin on a page with my reactions to compelling passages, sticky notes—especially the 1½-by-2-inch variety—force me to be concise. Usually, I jot down just a word or phrase or sometimes a question mark, a comma (for a passage that gives me pause), or an exclamation point (when I have a strong reaction). (I have adapted this approach into a full-blown strategy called the "punctuation prompt" in *The Book Club Companion*.) Making these brief notations doesn't significantly disrupt the flow of my reading. After all, the point—and this is what I tell my students—isn't to respond exhaustively but to write just enough to jog my thinking later when I want to elaborate further in writing, conversation, or both.

Sticky notes help students learn how to annotate without marring texts for future readers with marginalia, highlighting, or underlining. I show students my own sticky-noted books and talk about how the stickies help me remember, sometimes years later, what I was thinking at the time I read the book. By thinking aloud about a starter text we're reading together, I model not only how to use sticky notes but also how to do so judiciously. (Our dutiful over-achievers sometimes need permission to realize more isn't always better.) Beth asks her students to try for three sticky notes per reading, describing the notes as a "place for holding your thinking" until discussing these thoughts with oth-ers. Another thing I like about sticky notes is their portability. Selecting a few sticky notes to transfer to another piece of paper (like dailies) forces students to prioritize which thoughts deserve further development through writing and conversation.

Modeling working with sticky notes helps students use them purposefully. Beth uses the following procedure with the first starter text in a CDS. She intro-duces sticky notes by explaining her rationale for using them in her personal reading and then reads some brief comments she has written on sticky notes in one of her own books. Next, she distributes three or four sticky notes to each stu-dent along with their first starter text, a short story by Horacio Quiroga called "The Son." (This eerie story is told from the point of view of a single father who fears the consequences of allowing his young son to go hunting with a friend in a nearby forest. Its ambiguous ending never fails to provoke discussion, making it an especially good starter text.) Depending on the needs of a particular class, Beth reads this story aloud or asks student volunteers to do a "popcorn" reading. Unlike round-robin reading, during popcorn reading, volunteers read a portion of the text they feel comfortable reading, usually one or more paragraphs. When one volunteer stops reading, another student begins. The first time students try popcorn reading, you may want to identify volunteers at the beginning and write their names on the board so that everyone knows who will read next. Eventually students just pause for a moment before another volunteer begins reading spontaneously.

Well aware of the drawbacks of traditional round-robin reading (students often zone out until their turn comes; the quality of reading suffers when struggling or unwilling students are required to read; and so on), I was skepti-cal when Beth wanted to use popcorn reading with a starter text. What I dis-covered after seeing her do so with several classes is that the students who volunteer *enjoy* reading aloud and almost always do so beautifully, uninten-tionally modeling how to read fluently and with expression. I now use popcorn reading in my own classes occasionally because it fulfills what I think has always been the intent of round-robin reading: allowing a class to have a shared reading experience.

If you think reading the text aloud yourself will be more effective, use it as an opportunity to model thinking aloud. Prior to reading the story to your students, select a few strategic stopping points. Then while you're reading the story aloud, stop reading at the places you've designated and orally share your thinking. I've also seen Beth use these stopping places to model how to use sticky notes. She pauses at a particular point in the story, speaks aloud what she is writing on her sticky note, and explains why she is making this readerly move. For instance, when reading "The Son" aloud, she might say:

> You know, one of the things I do as a reader is ask questions while I'm reading. In this part of the story, I'm starting to wonder what is actually happening and what is only happening in the father's mind. The narrator keeps using words like *vision* and *illusion*. Is the father hallucinating? I'm going to write that question on my sticky note so I can ask someone else what they think.

Sometimes Beth simply notes her reactions, writing a word like *confusing* on a sticky note or recording a question that she hopes will be answered later in the story. Other times she makes observations that make her emerging understanding of a character clear. She may also mark a passage that seems especially important or beautifully written or a word she needs to look up later.

Modeling how to use sticky notes not only allows you to map your reading processes for students but also shows them how you deal with the four kinds of textual difficulty (Steiner 1978; see Figure 4.1). In "The Son," for instance, you might pose the following questions and think aloud about what you would do as a reader to answer them:

- "What does *yacutoro* mean? I'll look this word up later." (Contingent difficulty, dealing with denotative meaning of a word)

- "Why is the description of nature getting more negative as the story goes on? I'll just keep reading and maybe I'll figure it out." (Modal difficulty, since in a short story this progression parallels the rising action)

- "Why does the narrator shift between talking *about* the father and talking from the father's point of view? Maybe he is trying to give us an outside perspective and get inside the father's head to see *and* feel his panic because he can't find his son." (Tactical difficulty, demonstrating how the author's stylistic choices shape the reader's response to the text)

■ "Why would a father give a thirteen-year-old a shotgun and let him go out in the forest alone? I would never let my son do this." (Ontological difficulty, reflecting differences between the character's and reader's view of the world)

Remember that you will want to model only a few of your thoughts. Beth only marks three or four stopping places; stopping more frequently can disrupt the flow of the reading and overwhelm students with options. In fact, she often thinks aloud only about the first couple of sticky notes; in the remaining places she asks students to use a sticky note in a way that makes sense to them.

Whether Beth reads the starter text aloud or orchestrates a popcorn reading, she uses the resulting sticky notes to prompt a whole-class discussion. She briefly notes students' sticky-note responses on a three-column transparency—"student," "sticky-note response," and "readerly move." After the discussion has wound down, Beth fills in the third column, identifying the kind of contribution each student has made (see Figure 4.2).

Figure 4.2 - Beth's Transparency on Class Discussion of "The Son"

Student	Sticky-Note Response	Readerly Move
Leticia	13-year-old with a gun?	Personal reaction
R.C.	Foreshadowing	Attention to setting
Robby	Something bad is about to go down	Personal reaction
Zane	Hallucinations	Tracing plot
R.C.	Does it say why he hallucinates?	Clarifying question
Zane	"silver hair is drenched in sweat"—old people have hallucinations	Reacting to important quote/noticing details
Monica	Hallucinates, hears shot	Noticing details
Robby	"hope and faith lies in . . ."	Reacting to important quote/observing author's style
Caleb	Wants to believe, avoids the truth	Analyzing character

Thinking aloud about what you are writing on your sticky notes and asking students to share their responses makes visible the process that occurs when readers engage with texts and encounter challenges in making meaning.

Bookmarks

Once students have learned to respond to texts in open-ended ways using sticky notes, you can introduce the second element of the trio—the bookmark (see Figure 4.3). This elegant little tool has three panels: a reading schedule, a reminder of procedures for using sticky notes, and a list of response prompts. (Appendix B-1 provides instructions for constructing the bookmark.) I'll describe more about how the three panels work together in the next chapter.

Because students are reading starter texts at this point, they won't need to set a reading schedule. The second panel of the bookmark explains how to use it in conjunction with sticky notes, while the third panel contains a list of prompts. These prompts cue students to do four things:

1. Analyze characters in accessible ways

2. Identify and respond to controversial issues rather than shying away from them

3. Consider the cultural significance of such issues

4. Reflect on how their understanding of and response to the text is shaped by their personal experiences and background

Admittedly, the prompts constrain students' response options, but not inordinately. Students can still choose how they will respond, but the prompts push their thinking beyond "I like/didn't like this book," "I didn't understand this part," and "this character reminded me of. . . ." Don't get me wrong: in the book club conversations I've observed over the years, these topics inevitably appear, but they are familiar ground for most students, while discussing controversial issues productively isn't. The bookmark prompts are an important touchstone. As you help students practice using the prompts on starter texts, they get the exoscaffolding they need to use them independently with subsequent texts.

Dailies

The next layer of response is a two-sided form called "dailies," the third element of the trio. As the name suggests, students complete dailies regularly to prepare for discussion and to reflect on their participation. Dailies require students to (1) select

Figure 4.3 - Sticky-Notes Bookmark for High School Students

Reading Schedule	What's Up with the Sticky Notes	Sticky-Note Prompts (*Choose your own*)
By _____, we agreed to read to p. ___.	Since you chose this book, the hard part probably won't be reading it; the hard part will be stopping. But . . .	What are the most important **events** in this section of the book? Why are they the most important?
By _____, we agreed to read to p. ___.	You've agreed to talk about it; that's where the sticky notes come in. They let you mark the parts you'd like to talk about without slowing down your reading too much. **Here's how to use them:** 1. When you come to a part that you'd like to talk about with your group, peel off a sticky note to mark the page.	How do I feel about these **characters**? Close, distant, or somewhere in between? Why do I feel this way? What are the **most challenging or controversial conflicts, issues, or ideas** in this section of the book? Where do they come from? How do these conflicts and issues come up? How do they play out in the book?
By _____, we agreed to read to p. ___.	2. Use the reminders in the next column —> to help you decide why this passage is important.	What are the **characters' reactions** to these conflicts, issues, or ideas? What clues do these reactions give me about their personalities, motivations, and expectations for life?
By _____, we agreed to read to p. ___.	3. Then, jot down the page number and a short "note to self" directly on the sticky note so you'll remember the question/ comment/concern that prompted you to mark the passage in the first place. When your group meets, you can quickly review these sticky notes to decide which topics are the most important ones to focus on during your discussion.	What are *my reactions* to this section of the book? Do I feel detached? Connected? Skeptical? Confused? Something else? Why do I feel this way? How are my reactions to the issues and ideas this book raises shaped by my **personal experiences and background** (social class, gender, race, and so on)? By **other book club members' reactions and expectations?** **What** questions do I have about this section? What **important passages** did I notice? Why are they important?

a few of their sticky notes and elaborate on them in writing *prior to* discussion and (2) use metatalk to reflect on their group's and their own participation *after* discussion. Depending on the level of support students need with reflection, you may want to ask students to focus only on the first side of the form with starter texts. Later on when they are discussing a book-length text in small groups or book clubs, you can introduce the metatalk section. Appendix B-2 is a dailies form for high school students; Appendix B-3 is one for middle school students (the middle school version corresponds directly with the prompts on the middle school bookmark).

Visual Interpretation: An Optional Addendum

If visual representations will be included in students' final projects at the end of a CDS, you may want to supplement the trio of response strategies by letting students practice smaller-scale visual representations with a starter text the whole class has read. Once small groups have identified what they think is most important for others to understand about a text, they must condense and express their key interpretations in symbolic terms. Visual interpretations allow students to offer the individual observations they have recorded in dailies as fodder for group discussion. These activities work especially well as segues from teacher-facilitated discussion of whole-class texts to student-run discussions of multiple texts. Let me give you an example.

Right after her students had discussed two starter texts as a whole class but before they moved into book clubs to discuss the texts of their choice, Rebecca divided them into small groups to create visual interpretations of a long narrative poem, "The White Rose: Sophie Scholl," by Erika Mumford. This thirty-four-stanza poem spans the life of a young German girl who belonged to the White Rose, a small secret society that resisted the Nazi regime by anonymously distributing thousands of leaflets to scholars, medics, pub owners, and university students. The poem is difficult, so Rebecca told students they would divide their intellectual labor to interpret it. She asked them to read and sticky-note the entire poem before coming to class but to concentrate their dailies on assigned stanzas (some students were to focus on stanzas 1–5, others on stanzas 6–10, and so forth). The next day, they formed six groups according to their assigned segments of the poem, and Rebecca projected the guidelines for the activity on an overhead transparency:

- Draw four or five symbols that capture the most important aspects of your assigned section of the poem. These symbols *don't* have to mirror actual images in the poem, but they can.

- When you share your visual interpretation with the whole class, you'll need to explain *why* your group chose those particular symbols. This will be a way for us to discuss the poem as a whole.

- Also be thinking about what the big ideas and issues are in this poem as a whole. Why do these ideas/issues matter now? To you and to the world?

Students spent about half an hour discussing their section of the poem, deciding what symbols they wanted to use, and drawing their interpretations on panels of butcher paper. Rebecca then asked each group to post their panels at the front of the room and walk the class through their thinking. As each group presented, she asked clarifying questions and probed their responses as necessary so that students weren't just listing symbols but were explaining the reasoning behind them. When students weren't presenting, they jotted down notes and questions they wanted to raise during whole-class discussion. This approach prevented the bogging down that sometimes occurs when whole-class discuss follows each group's presentation. Asking students to take notes ensured that they paid attention to their classmates' presentations rather than zoning out until their group's turn. Because the discussion carried over to the next day, these notes also provided continuity and a detailed reminder of students' initial thoughts.

Richly grounded in the students' observations and questions, the whole-class discussion focused on the poem's most important and puzzling aspects. Displayed in order at the front of the room, the panels traced the poem's chronology and forced students to return to specific sections of the text when making a particular point. Returning to the final question in the activity toward the end of the discussion extended the poem's relevance beyond a distant moment in history by helping students make personal and universal connections to its content. In one remarkable discussion of the poem, students engaged in tough talk on such culturally significant topics as whether war is ever justified, if peace is possible, and if small gestures like Sophie Scholl's acts of resistance matter when one's ultimate goal is beyond reach (such as ending a war). This activity prepared students well for the visual interpretation project they would complete at the conclusion of their book club discussions and was concrete proof of the power of collaborative thinking.

Putting It All Together

There is no exact algorithm for combining response tools in order to prepare students to independently engage in tough talk. Beth, Cameron, and Rebecca pick and choose among them as appropriate for any given class. Figure 4.4 provides examples of how they have combined the tools in particular instances. Each example explains the focus of the class, the tools that were introduced, and the starter texts that were used.

Figure 4.4 - Putting It All Together

Beth's Multiage English Class at an Alternative High School	
DAY ONE	
Focus	Establish civil discourse norms; introduce quickwrites and sticky notes; discuss first starter text
Tools	• Quickwrite to the following prompt: *We talk a lot about effective communication skills, but what does it look like to use them? Write about a time you used your communication skills effectively when discussing a controversial or potentially upsetting topic.* • Debriefing discussions of quickwrite and starter text • Sticky notes
Starter Text	"The Son" (short story by Horacio Quiroga), marked with designated stopping places
DAY TWO	
Focus	Reinforce norms and response tools; introduce second starter text; begin discussion of second starter text in small groups
Tools	• Quickwrite to the following prompt: *What do you do when a loved one wants to do something risky? Do you let them, or do you say no to keep them safe?* • Debriefing discussions of quickwrite and starter text • Sticky notes
Starter Text	"Spear" (short story by Julian Lester)
DAY THREE	
Focus	Establish norms for book clubs; introduce sticky-notes bookmark
Tools	• Sticky-notes bookmark • What Is *Civil Discourse*? handout • Quickwrite to the following prompt: *Respond to the scenarios on the handout. Brainstorm some solutions.* • Book Club Goals and Ground Rules handout (see Chapter 5)
Starter Text	——

Figure 4.4 - Putting It All Together (continued)

	Rebecca's Tenth-Grade Pre-AP English Class at a Suburban High School
DAY ONE	
Focus	Introduce civil discourse and sticky notes; establish small-group civil discourse norms; assign first starter text
Tools	• What Is *Civil Discourse*? handout • Book Club Goals and Ground Rules handout (see Chapter 5) • Sticky notes
Starter Text	——-
DAY TWO	
Focus	Discuss first starter text; introduce dailies; assign second starter text
Tools	Dailies
Starter Text	"The Son" (short story by Horacio Quiroga)
DAY THREE	
Focus	Discuss second starter text in small groups; assign third starter text and provide its historical context
Tools	PowerPoint presentation on historical context of "The White Rose: Sophie Scholl"
Starter Text	"Spear" (short story by Julian Lester)
DAY FOUR	
Focus	Discuss second starter text as a class; visually interpret third starter text in small groups
Tools	Visual interpretation
Starter Text	"The White Rose: Sophie Scholl" (long poem on the Holocaust by Erika Mumford)
DAY FIVE	
Focus	Complete small-group visual interpretations and present them to the class
Tools	Visual interpretation
Starter Text	"The White Rose" (continued)
DAY SIX	
Focus	Finish visual interpretation presentations; establish book club norms; introduce sticky-notes bookmarks
Tools	• Visual interpretation (continued) • Book Club Goals and Ground Rules handout (see Chapter 5) • Sticky-notes bookmark
Starter Text	"The White Rose" (continued)

Figure 4.4 - Putting It All Together (continued)

<table>
<tr><td colspan="2" align="center">Two of Cameron's Sixth-Grade Classes at a Rural Elementary School *Variation One*</td></tr>
<tr><td colspan="2">**DAY ONE**</td></tr>
<tr><td>*Focus*</td><td>Introduce civil discourse; present book talk on first starter text; discuss first starter text</td></tr>
<tr><td>*Tools*</td><td>Discussion questions</td></tr>
<tr><td>*Starter Text*</td><td>"Waiting on the World to Change" (song lyrics by John Mayer)</td></tr>
<tr><td colspan="2">**DAY TWO**</td></tr>
<tr><td>*Focus*</td><td>Define "controversy"; introduce sticky-notes bookmark; establish book club norms</td></tr>
<tr><td>*Tools*</td><td>

- Quickwrite
- Debriefing discussion of quickwrites
- Sticky-notes bookmark
- Book Club Goals and Ground Rules handout (see Chapter 5)
</td></tr>
<tr><td colspan="2" align="center">*Variation Two (for students who need more practice with starter texts prior to civil discourse book clubs)*</td></tr>
<tr><td colspan="2">**DAY ONE (two weeks prior to start of civil discourse book clubs)**</td></tr>
<tr><td>*Focus*</td><td>Introduce book clubs; present book talks on starter texts</td></tr>
<tr><td>*Tools*</td><td>——-</td></tr>
<tr><td>*Starter Texts*</td><td>*Hatchet* (Paulsen), *Walk Two Moons* (Creech), *Gifts* (Le Guin)</td></tr>
<tr><td colspan="2">**DAY TWO**</td></tr>
<tr><td>*Focus*</td><td>Introduce sticky-notes bookmark; establish book club norms; begin reading starter texts</td></tr>
<tr><td>*Tools*</td><td>

- Sticky-notes bookmark
- Book Club Goals and Ground Rules handout (see Chapter 5)
</td></tr>
<tr><td>*Starter Texts*</td><td>Same as above</td></tr>
<tr><td colspan="2">**DAY THREE**</td></tr>
<tr><td>*Focus*</td><td>Introduce dailies and Book Club Discussion Record; begin discussing starter texts in book clubs</td></tr>
<tr><td>*Tools*</td><td>

- Dailies
- Book Club Discussion Record handout (see Chapter 5)
</td></tr>
<tr><td>*Starter Texts*</td><td>Same as above</td></tr>
<tr><td colspan="2">**DAYS FOUR–TEN**</td></tr>
<tr><td>*Focus*</td><td>Discuss starter texts in book clubs</td></tr>
<tr><td>*Tools*</td><td>

- Dailies
- Book Club Discussion Record handout (see Chapter 5)
</td></tr>
<tr><td>*Starter Texts*</td><td>Same as above</td></tr>
</table>

Tough Talk, Tough Texts

Figure 4.4 - Putting It All Together (continued)

DAY ELEVEN (start of civil discourse book clubs)	
Focus	Introduce civil discourse and first starter text; discuss first starter text
Tools	Discussion questions
Starter Text	"Waiting on the World to Change" (song lyrics by John Mayer)
DAY TWELVE	
Focus	Define "controversy"; establish norms for civil discourse book clubs; begin reading the civil discourse book
Tools	• Quickwrite • Debriefing discussion • Book Club Goals and Ground Rules handout (see Chapter 5) • Sticky-notes bookmark
Starter Text	——-

Although their daily procedures differ, you can see how Beth, Cam, and Rebecca provide exoscaffolding for their students so they will have a sturdy framework for their small-group discussions of book-length tough texts. As they move into small-group talk, however, students require continued support. In your classroom, too, scaffolding must be perpetual, though from this point on in the CDS, it will differ in kind as well as degree. The next chapter shows you how to help students sustain tough talk—that most "seriously neglected" skill in school (Probst 2007).

Chapter 5

*Every time I see an adult on a bicycle
I no longer despair for the human
race.*

—H. G. WELLS

Up to this point, we've provided a significant amount of exoscaffolding for students, helping them set up class discussion norms, define civil discourse, and practice it with starter texts. Now it's time to let students go it alone in small groups or book clubs. You may be wondering, *Why not just continue this approach as a whole class?* For the same reason you don't run alongside children forever as they're learning to ride a bike. Your legs will give out, your arms will get tired, and besides, kids need to find their own way without you. This chapter is about letting go of the bicycle seat, about equipping students with the resources and strategies they will need to transfer their knowledge about tough talk from the classroom to the world outside.

Sustaining Civil Discourse

In *Going with the Flow: How to Engage Boys (and Girls) in Their Literacy Learning* (2006), Michael Smith and Jeff Wilhelm describe how infrequently adolescent boys use what they learn in school in their lives outside school. Their interviews with boys make the prospect that students will transfer knowledge from text to text, class to class, or school to world seem pretty dismal. However, they cite the work of Robert Haskell (2000), who maintains that transfer can occur if the following conditions are met:

1. Students have command of the *knowledge* that is to be transferred.

2. Students have a *theoretical understanding* of the principles to be transferred.

3. The *classroom culture* cultivates a spirit of transfer.

4. Students get plenty of *practice.*

(Smith and Wilhelm 2006, 26, emphasis mine)

In other words, assuming students will transfer what they learn just because *we* see the relevance of our instruction for other tasks and settings is magical thinking. Similarly, the ultimate motivation for our teaching cannot be that students should learn something now because they will need to know it someday—in the next grade, in college, or in the "real world." In truth, don't we want them to learn something they can use now *and* later? Don't we want the best of both worlds for our students? And who's to say that school isn't the "real world" for students, considering that that they spend the bulk of their days there for at least a good thirteen years? If this is the case, we must provide explicit support so that the transfer of knowledge and skills can take place.

The strategies and procedures in this chapter meet all of Haskell's criteria for transfer. They help students develop firsthand knowledge of *what* civil discourse is, know *why* it's important, understand the *relevance* of this knowledge both inside and outside the classroom, and *apply* that knowledge deliberately and often. Your students will be familiar with many of these strategies because you've already introduced them with starter texts, but now it's time to combine them and apply them to a book-length text. In doing so, students will learn how to sustain civil discourse on their own.

Some Preliminary Decisions: Choosing Texts and Grouping Students

You have two options from this point forward: either teach a common text that all students will read and discuss in small groups or have students form book clubs and choose from a range of texts. In the first instance, you'll have more decisions to make about grouping students; in the second, you'll have more decisions to make about choosing texts. There are valid practical and pedagogical reasons for either choice.

When to Use a Common Text
Even though Beth, Cam, Rebecca, and I conducted our research in a book club setting, other teachers adapt these strategies and use them with a common text.

I've used the common-text approach in my university classroom and in an after-hours high school book club for which students read *East of Eden.* Choosing a common text makes sense when you are confined to the books available at your school, your curriculum dictates the literature you must teach, a text is more difficult than students can handle completely on their own, or all the above, but you still want students to have an independent experience with the text.

Classics that meet the criteria for tough texts that I talked about in Chapter 2 often fall in this category. My own experience reading *The Grapes of Wrath* as a high school student is a good example of when a common text would be in order. Without question, this novel qualifies as a tough text. Stunning in its literary complexity, it's also chock-full of culturally significant issues and compelling characters wrestling with difficult choices. But when I was sixteen, that's not why I decided to read it.

At the start of my junior year, the high school librarian distributed a list of classic texts that all college-bound students should read. Determined to prepare myself for college, I decided to read as many of the books as I could before I graduated. I must have reasoned that the thicker the book, the more knowledge I would gain, because I headed straight for *The Grapes of Wrath.* Even though I was an avid reader, the novel was a tough row to hoe. I could follow along with the Joads on their trek to California just fine, but I couldn't figure out why Steinbeck devoted big chunks of the text, whole chapters even, to little things that didn't seem important to the plot, like the turtle's journey across the highway in Chapter 3.

After many years of teaching, I now know that even advanced readers can struggle with a particular text—think W–4 form, prescription drug insert, or *The Faerie Queene.* The chief difference between independent and dependent readers, however, is that independent readers know what to do when they encounter a difficult text (Beers 2002). They might stop and reread a passage they don't understand, for instance, or take another look at context to determine the meaning of an unfamiliar word or ask a more experienced reader or a teacher for help.

Even though I was an independent reader captivated by Steinbeck's epic story line in eleventh grade, I wasn't nerdy enough to seek my English teacher's help with a book I was reading alone, no matter how tough the going. I was determined, however, to check another title off my list of classics, so I eventually gave up and "read around" the turtle passage and others I knew I wasn't quite getting, like the ending of the novel, for which I was emotionally unprepared. Without a doubt, I know I would have had a deeper, more satisfying experience with the book if I'd had a teacher's help in grasping its metaphorical significance.

Novels like *The Grapes of Wrath* make good common texts because they allow teachers to adopt a "big-chunk/little-chunk" approach in their instruction (Gallagher 2009, 99), letting students read long portions of the text that they can handle independently and guiding them through short sections where they can use more help (e.g., the metaphorically driven sections like Steinbeck's turtle passage). Using little chunks of text, teachers can model their reading processes with think-alouds, provide historical context or vocabulary support, or ask students to read with a particular focus. Students will still get independent practice with civil discourse by discussing the big chunks together.

How to Group Students When Using a Common Text

If you decide to use a common text, your options for dividing students into small discussion groups include random selection, your selection, student selection, or some combination.

To select students randomly you could ask students to number off or use some other method like Tracey Rosewarne recommends in *Purposeful Writing* (Sipe and Rosewarne 2006). When organizing students into initial writing groups, she distributes a pack of playing cards and asks them to assemble in ranks (that is, all the 2s together, the 4s together, and so on). Random selection ensures some heterogeneity and often allows students to work with others who don't sit near them, a bonus if you want to break up cliques and perhaps expose students to more varied perspectives. If you use this method, students may need more time to settle in with classmates they might not know as well as the friends they sit next to in class, especially since they'll be discussing the culturally sensitive topics inherent in tough texts. Incorporating an activity or two to help small groups get acquainted, providing extra support when establishing norms, or even asking groups to work through a short starter text together can increase students' comfort level.

Another option for grouping students is for you to do so. This method guarantees heterogeneity because it allows you to keep social dynamics, learning styles, and work habits of individual students in mind. If you choose this option, I urge you to avoid ability grouping, however. At first glance, ability grouping may make intuitive sense. You may think, for instance, that the higher achievers will push one another or that you'll be better able to differentiate instruction by providing the less able students with more support. But let's call the practice what it is—tracking—and students are able to spot it a mile away. Tracking imposes an academic caste system and perpetuates existing social inequities, especially because an inordinate number of students of color are often relegated to the lowest ranks (see Christensen 2000; Oakes 2005; Rose 2005). Joan Cone's teacher research (2003) describes the challenges and rewards of untracking her AP English class and makes clear that when teachers group students—whether in class or in the school as whole—they should do so with care.

Another grouping option is to let students choose. Students are likely to choose others with whom they are compatible and therefore comfortable discussing difficult issues. On the other hand, groups can become cliques that reinforce existing inequitable power structures. When students get *too* comfortable working with their pals, they may gloss over differences of opinion for fear of jeopardizing their social capital, thus limiting their access to varied perspectives (Finders 1997). Timing may also play a part; student choice may be more important toward the beginning of the year when the intimacy of existing friendships may help students take more interpretive risks.

The final option is to use some combination of the above methods. I most often combine the last two. For instance, I'll ask students to list two or three classmates with whom they'd like to work, then make the final decisions based on their suggestions, my knowledge of social dynamics, and my desire to expand students' perspectives through heterogeneous grouping. Because every option has benefits and drawbacks, I try to use all of them at some point in the year, giving students a range of opportunities for collaborative learning.

When to Use Book Clubs

When you have curricular flexibility and access to a variety of texts, I suggest using book clubs. I have interviewed class after class of Beth's, Cam's, and Rebecca's students. Every one of them recommended that English teachers use book clubs, and choice was their number one reason. If you imagine going into your favorite bookstore and seeing every shelf stocked with a single title, you'll understand why students yearn for some say in what they are expected to read in school.

In many classrooms, reading workshop and sustained silent reading are opportunities for students to incorporate more choice into their individual reading. While these are sound practices, I firmly believe students need shared reading experience, too. Even as an adult reader, I understand literary texts differently after discussing them with my book club and feel challenged by the thoughts of colleagues when we read professional texts together. Shared reading experiences ensure that my students will be similarly stretched.

Choosing from a menu of book titles also increases the likelihood that students will continue developing a reader identity. In fact, the menu is a good metaphor for what Richard Allington (2007) refers to as "managed choice." Just as a restaurant limits diners' choices to a few good dishes rather than overwhelming them with a list of all possible culinary creations, you manage students' choices by pulling together a small menu of texts and letting them choose one to read in a book club. Students benefit from your expertise in forming the menu, but they also figure out who they are as readers by making their own decisions about the books they want to read.

How to Group Students in Book Clubs

The greatest determining factor for placing students in book clubs is their book preference. Once you have selected the books, you can rely on students' reading preferences and your sense of social dynamics to determine how students will be grouped. The tough texts you choose for book clubs should meet the criteria I described in Chapter 3, with the caveat that you'll be unlikely to include especially difficult texts like *The Grapes of Wrath* in the mix. (Think back to my encounter with Steinbeck's turtle.)

You'll give a booktalk describing each tough text so that students can make a ranked list of their top choices. Booktalks are short, only a couple of minutes per book, and typically contain five elements:

1. *Plot overview.* Provide enough information about the main characters, conflict, and setting to intrigue students but not enough to give the story away. If you think of a booktalk as a verbal movie trailer, you should find the right balance.

2. *A brief passage read-aloud.* Find two or three paragraphs you think will simultaneously hook students and give them a feel for the narrator's voice and the pace of the book.

3. *Additional information of interest.* Mention awards the book has won, relevant facts about the author, and the like. It's easy to get carried away here, so choose a couple of items that you think *students* might find interesting.

4. *List of controversial aspects.* Without sensationalizing, make students aware of tough topics, issues, and/or language the book contains so they will be able to choose a book they will feel comfortable reading and discussing.

5. *Single-sentence wrap-up.* Leave students with one important thing to remember about the book. Try lines like:

   ■ *If you like [similar book/movie/author/genre], this book is for you.*

   ■ *This book will make you [think/cry/question/and so on] because . . .*

   ■ *I chose this book for book clubs because . . .*

   ■ *After one of my previous students read this book, s/he said . . .*

If students are making their book choices right after your booktalks, you may want to pass each book around after you describe it. If you're going to let them sleep on it, prop the books on the chalk tray and give them a few minutes at the end of class to thumb through them. I sometimes distribute a handout that lists each book along with a two- or three-sentence annotation and a downloaded JPG image of the cover. There are many great resources that will help you prepare booktalks (several are listed in Appendix A-2); most include summaries, special features, age appropriateness, and suggestions for passages to read aloud.

After your booktalk, ask students to list their top three choices (or top two if you're offering only four books), explaining that although all students won't get their first pick, you'll do your best to make sure they get one of their top choices. This isn't an empty promise. It feels a little like magic, but in all my years of using book clubs in my classroom, I've always been able to honor one of every student's top requests, as have Beth, Cam, and Rebecca. You will, too.

Because it is already constrained by their book choices, sorting students into book clubs is surprisingly quick and easy. I can usually list the members of various book clubs on the board within minutes while students are completing another brief task. After collecting students' ranked lists, I first do a rough sort by title, putting all the first choices for a particular title in one stack, all the first choices for another title in a second stack, and so on. Next, I start with the *smallest* stack. Since these students will definitely get their first choice, I now need to fill out the group with other students who have listed this book as their second choice. Once the group is filled, I move on to the second smallest stack and go through the same process with the rest of the titles until all the groups are filled. Group sizes may vary depending on title popularity and that's fine, as long as groups are no larger than six (it's easy for students to get lost in the shuffle during discussion if they are) and no smaller than four (in book clubs with three or fewer students, it can be difficult to carry on a sustained discussion or hear a variety of perspectives, especially if someone is absent). If you have enough copies, it's also okay to have more than one book club reading the same book.

As I'm sorting, I also keep social dynamics in mind, considering which students will work best together and who might challenge whom in productive ways. In the past, I intentionally tried to avoid explosive combinations at all costs, but Cam's sixth graders have challenged my thinking. During a whole-class interview, I asked if they had any advice for teachers who wanted to use book clubs in their classrooms. One student suggested that compatibility among students shouldn't be the number one priority when forming groups. He said, "I think teachers should put kids who don't always agree in the same group so they can learn to get along. I mean, isn't that what civil discourse is for?" This kid got it. Since then, my goal hasn't been to avoid potential confrontations in book clubs so much as it has been to help students work through them if and when they occur.

Whether you're using book clubs or everyone is reading a common text, the support you give students from now on is different from that you provided with starter texts. So far, you've used lots of exoscaffolding, introducing students to the concept of civil discourse and giving them practice with several response strategies. You'll now shift primarily to *endoscaffolding*, providing support *within* small groups as students discuss their book-length text. Your support remains perpetual throughout the CDS, but from this point on your role shifts in two important ways: (1) it becomes more contextually based, in that you're tailoring support for each small group *at the point of need*, and (2) it becomes more implicit so that students can use civil discourse independently.

The Elements of a Civil Discourse Sequence

The following sections describe all the elements of a CDS students will now use independently and provide examples of endoscaffolding.

Establishing Norms

Once small groups or book clubs are established, students will need to establish norms and determine a reading schedule. If you used the scenarios on the What

Is *Civil Discourse?* handout from Chapter 1 to set class norms with starter texts, now is the time to refer back to these norms. While students shouldn't feel bound to copy them exactly, reviewing the list will give them a starting point for establishing norms in their small groups.

Cam doesn't use What Is *Civil Discourse?* at all with his sixth graders because he prefers to work on norms throughout book clubs, using quickwrites and debriefing discussions to deepen his middle school students' understanding of civil discourse while they are in the process of using it. Here's a day-by-day account of how this approach looks in his classroom:

> *Day 1:* Students, in small groups, analyze song lyrics[1] as a starter text and quickwrite about the social problems the lyrics reveal; then they discuss potential solutions as a whole class.

> *Day 2:* This session focuses entirely on defining and dealing with controversy. Throughout the period, Cam asks students to complete a multi-prompt quickwrite, sandwiching debriefing discussions between each prompt.
>
> First, students spend about three minutes defining the word *controversy*. Students' definitions usually vary widely, though most initially see controversy as decidedly negative, as the following excerpts illustrate:

- *Controversy is sometimes a selfish argument. Just people sharing their feelings about something and making a big deal out of it.*

- *Controversy to me is something I need to get over.*

- *Controversy is wild, fighting. Controversy is just crazy things that happen.*

- *Controversy . . . is a way to show violence and sometimes can get a person killed.*

- *Something controversial is when people fight for food. Who gets the last piece of chicken, who gets the last Coke, who eats the pizza, who lets the pizza go stone cold. It's all stupid.*

---

[1] Cam has used "Waiting on the World to Change," by John Mayer, for this activity, but other songs with relevant themes include "I'll Go Crazy If I Don't Go Crazy Tonight," by U2, "Handlebars," by Flobots, "Where Is the Love?" by the Black Eyed Peas, "Man in the Mirror," by Michael Jackson, and, of course, "Revolution," by the Beatles.

After a debriefing discussion in which students share ideas from their quickwrites and compare their responses to a dictionary definition, Cam asks them to write again.

For the second three-minute quickwrite, they fill out a T-chart that lists effective ways of handling controversy in the left column, ineffective ways in the right. In the debriefing discussion afterward, he compiles a class list and points out that some items, such as "stay away from the subject" or "leave the room" show up on both sides of the chart. He asks students why they think this is and sends them back to the dictionary to look up the words *disagree* and *argue*. They flesh out these definitions by discussing how the body language people use when they disagree differs from their body language when they argue and then considering the personal and public consequences of either course.

In the final quickwrite on day 2, students write to this prompt: *When something comes up that makes you uncomfortable during book club, what are the good and bad things you can do in your group to help you talk about it? This time as you write, focus especially on the effective ways of dealing with controversy.* Here's a representative response:

> *When you are disagreeing you are not yelling and screaming. You are not being loud. You just sit there and say I think it goes this way. You just talk. You just tell the other person what you think and why without yelling or anything. It is just like a discussion.*

In the space of a couple of class periods, students have moved from considering general definitions of controversy, disagreement, and argument to making personal action plans they can apply in their small-group discussions.

Day 3: Students meet in book clubs to set their norms, then spend the rest of the period reading their books.

As you can see, Cam provides lots of exoscaffolding before students break into their book clubs to prepare them for setting norms, but if he notices a common problem after students have started discussing their books, he asks everyone to quickwrite about alternative courses of action. After the quickwrite, students underline the "most profound thing" they put down and share these insights in a quick read-around while Cam records them on the board. After the class discusses which solutions seem to be the most viable and why, he asks them to quickwrite about how they personally will apply these solutions in future book club discussions.

You too can use quickwrites and debriefing discussions to help book clubs follow their own norms. Resist the well-meaning urge to dictate solutions to students' problems. Instead, help students generate solutions on their own that are immediately applicable in their groups and in their lives beyond the classroom.

Whether you frontload norming as Beth and Rebecca do or extend it throughout the CDS as Cam does, the Goals and Ground Rules handout (Figure 5.1) helps students assume responsibility for how they will run their group. Students complete this handout at their first official book club or small-group meeting. Their first task is to choose a group name. Although this task may seem inconsequential, it unites students in a playful mission, as these examples show:

- *Cam's students:* The Flaming Bunnies, Pink-Polka-Dotted Penguins, Champions

- *Beth's students:* Mythbusters, Teenage Mutant Ninja Turtledoves, The All-Knowing Venom-Spitting Mongooses

- *Rebecca's students:* Purple Cobras, Team Awesome, Key Lime with a Hint of Pumpkin

The handout also requires students to negotiate leadership roles right away and designate the day's discussion leader and scribe. Even though these roles rotate from meeting to meeting, this important first step prepares students for the routine. Next, students devise goals and ground rules to guide their subsequent group interactions. Putting these norms in writing produces a useful reference to help students honor their own intentions and hold one another accountable should breaches occur. Students then sign their names, cuing them to think of the agreement as a binding contract they have created collaboratively and will now together enforce. (If they are working in book clubs, students' final task is to decide their reading schedule and record it on their sticky-notes bookmark; I discuss this tool in the next section.)

By now it should be clear to students that you expect them to take agency for their actions from the very beginning of their discussions in small groups or

Book you're reading:_____

Members of your group:_____

Name for your group (create one! ☺):_____

Today's discussion leader:_____ Today's scribe:_____

GOALS: Talk about what an ideal group looks like to you and then set some goals (no more than 3 or 4) to help you become that group. List these goals below:

1. _____

2. _____

3. _____

4. _____

GROUND RULES: You'll have about half an hour to discuss your book each time. How do you want that time to be spent? Below, make a short list of ground rules (no more than 4 or 5) to guide how your group will work together. Some questions to consider are:

• How do you expect people to prepare for discussion?

• How do you want the discussion to proceed?

• How can you make sure people treat one another with honor and respect?

• What should your group do when someone isn't following these ground rules?

1. _____

2. _____

3. _____

4. _____

SIGNATURES: By signing below, you indicate your willingness to abide by the above agreement.

_____

_____

Figure 5.1 - Book Club Goals and Ground Rules

book clubs. Equalizing power dynamics disrupts the traditional teacher-student hierarchy, requiring you to assume a new role as well—the perfect opportunity for endoscaffolding. You might circulate among groups to ensure that their lists of norms are as concrete as possible. When Beth saw one group writing *show respect* as one of their norms, for instance, she dropped in and asked students to think about what showing respect looks like and sounds like. After talking it over, the group decided that showing respect meant to "talk one at a time" and "keep our discussions confidential."

You'll continue endoscaffolding for the rest of the CDS. If you keep these moments brief and to the point, you'll help students engage in tough talk independent of you and increase the chances that they will transfer this valuable skill beyond your classroom.

The Sticky-Notes Bookmark and Sticky Notes

After small groups have set their norms, they are ready to begin reading and responding to their books. Having already used sticky notes, the bookmark, and dailies with starter texts, students should be basically familiar with how these tools work. As they begin using them with a book-length text, however, you'll need to remind them how the strategies work together as a system. Let's review the sticky notes bookmark one panel at a time.

Panel 1: Reading Schedule. Because students have been reading starter texts up to now, they'll be the least familiar with this portion of the bookmark. They need to set reading deadlines so that everyone will have read to a certain page by an agreed-on date. This will help students pace their independent reading and be prepared for discussion.

If the class is reading a common text, there are three options for establishing common deadlines:

1. Divide the number of pages by the number of times students will meet in small groups to discuss the book (for example, if a book is 200 pages long and students are scheduled to meet four times, they will need to read 50 pages before each meeting).

2. Determine optimal stopping places for each meeting that probably won't correspond to an exact number of pages. For instance, you may want students to read fewer pages early on so that they can focus more

closely on the exposition, especially if there are details that will be crucial to understanding the story later. This option also allows you to schedule reading according to natural breaks in the text (e.g., transitions between major plot occurrences) and to use the "big chunk/little chunk" method (Gallagher 2009) as necessary.

3. Allow the class to negotiate a schedule that feels manageable to them. You still decide the number of small-group meetings, but they get to decide how many pages to read for each one. Even with a common text, if you don't see instructional advantages in having all groups adhere to the same schedule, leaving it up to the students is another way to reinforce their agency.

If students are reading books in book clubs, I recommend option 3. This allows groups to take their personal schedules into consideration. They may have a good reason to bulk up their reading one week and read fewer pages the next—school events, homework in other classes, after-school jobs. This option also allows them to honor chapter breaks. Reviewing the reading schedules groups determine is another opportunity for endoscaffolding. You can check back with groups whose schedules look off-balance, hear the rationale for their decisions, and troubleshoot as necessary.

Panel 2: Instructions for Sticky Notes. The second panel of the bookmark reminds students how to use sticky notes during their independent reading. You may want to warn them about the "highlighter phenomenon." Something about having a highlighter in your hand can make everything seem important so that before you know it, you've highlighted an entire passage or chapter. Now *everything* seems important, so you're no better off than you were before you used the highlighter in the first place. It's just as easy for students to fall prey to this phenomenon when they use sticky notes, so limiting the number they can use in one sitting helps them be more selective. Cam and Beth ask their students to limit to six the number of sticky notes they use during a single reading.

You can also suggest ways readers use sticky notes without disrupting the flow of their reading. Some readers like to jot down a few thoughts on the sticky note at the moment they mark a passage. Others like to mark potential passages (either with a sticky note or with some kind of symbol in the margin), then go back later to narrow down the passages that seem most important and comment on them then. Encourage students to find the method that works best for them.

Also remind students that they're only jotting down a few words or a brief phrase, not a comprehensive response. The time to elaborate will come later, on their dailies. Using the smaller 1½-by-2-inch sticky notes reinforces this message, but you can also share a few student examples or from your own reading (especially if you're using larger sticky notes). The following responses from Cam's students demonstrate a typical and appropriate length (I've listed the book title in parentheses after each comment):

- This proves women can do anything guys can do. (*Bridge to Terabithia*)

- What would you do if your mom died? (*Gathering Blue*)

- Why would you want to be in a group where they named you "Snots"? (*Wringer*)

- I love how the author put it—"a fierce blue." It is so descriptive. (*Heaven*)

- Tough stuff—Leslie's death is hard to talk about. (*Bridge to Terabithia*)

Panel 3: Prompts for Sticky Notes. The prompts on the third panel of the bookmark give students lots of options for how to use their sticky notes. Especially at the high school level, students often analyze structure (plot, conflict, character, and so on) and make connections with texts as a matter of course because that's what they've learned to do in prior grades. It's fine and important that they continue to do so, and some of the prompts on the bookmarks allow students to analyze characters and make emotional connections to the text. However, it's equally important that they consider and interrogate what's going on when they *aren't* making connections. Therefore, other prompts push students to consider the source of their response rather than simply assume, for instance, that they are connecting with a book because it's inherently "good" or aren't connecting with it because it's "flawed."

Instead of ignoring the parts of the text that challenge their understanding, students can use these prompts to tackle the range of difficulties readers encounter, especially ontological difficulties (Steiner 1978). You'll recall from Chapter 4 that ontological difficulties, such as understanding the validity of an author's or character's perspective, are the most challenging. These prompts from the high school bookmark (see Figure 4.3) challenge readers to tackle ontological issues:

- What are the *most challenging or controversial conflicts, issues, or ideas* in this section of the book? Where do they come from? How do these conflicts and issues come up? How do they play out in the book?

- What are the *characters' reactions* to [challenging or controversial] conflicts, issues, or ideas? What clues do these reactions give me about their personalities, motivations, and expectations for life?

- What are *my reactions* to this section of the book? Do I feel detached? connected? skeptical? confused? something else? Why do I feel this way?

- How are my reactions to the issues and ideas this book raises shaped by *my personal experiences and background* (social class, gender, race, and so on)? By *other book club members' reactions and expectations*?

The following prompts on the middle school bookmark (see Figure 5.2) are also designed to help students read empathically and consider varied world-views, but they are phrased in simpler language:

This part of the book made me . . .

- THINK about something I hadn't thought about before
- BLINK because I saw the world through the eyes of someone who is different from me
- NERVOUS because it challenged my way of thinking about something

As you remind students how to use the bookmark, encourage them to use their sticky notes with the end goal in mind—engaging in tough talk about tough texts. While prompts like those above are important to reach that goal, feel free to rewrite some of the other prompts to reflect your instructional focus. If you want to embed meaningful language study in students' reading, for instance, perhaps you'll ask them to highlight at least one "power word" with a sticky note—a word they are curious about, admire for its usage, or find interesting. These power words are then available for students to use in their own writing, as Sipe and Rosewarne (2006) recommend. Cam likewise encourages his students to employ their books as "mentor texts" by recording lines and passages they admire and would like to emulate (Anderson 2005). By reading like writers, stu-

Figure 5.2 - Bookmark for Middle School Students

My Official Sticky-Notes Bookmark	What's Up with the Sticky Notes?	This Part of the Book Made Me . . .
READING SCHEDULE By _____, read to p. ___. By _____, read to p. ___. By _____, read to p. ___. By _____, read to p. ___.	Since you chose this book, the hard part probably won't be reading it. The hard part will be stopping! But . . . You've agreed to talk about it! So you need to stop every so often and think about the parts that will help you remember what you think is important. And . . . That's where the sticky notes come in. They let you mark the parts you'd like to talk about in book club without slowing down your reading too much. **Here's how to use them:** 1. When you come to a part that you'd like to talk more about in book club, peel off a sticky note to mark the page. 2. Use the reminders in the next column → to help you decide what this part of the book made you do. 3. Then write down a short reminder for yourself directly on the sticky note. When you get back to book club, you'll use your sticky notes to help you decide what to talk about. That's all there is to it!	When writers decide to publish their work, they want to have an impact on their readers. As you read, think about what that part of the book is making you do as a reader. Then, write that word on your sticky note so that you can come back to it later in your dailies or in your book club discussion or both. Here are some prompts you can choose from: **THINK about something I hadn't thought about before** **BLINK because I saw the world through the eyes of someone who is different from me** **WONDER why an event happened or a character felt a certain way** **FEEL UNDERSTOOD because I could relate to a character or event** **LAUGH because something was really funny** ☺ **CRY because something was really sad** **CONFUSED because I just didn't understand what or why or how something could happen the way it did in the book** **NERVOUS because it challenged my way of thinking about something**

dents not only address the "contingent" difficulties in texts but also apprentice themselves to authors and eventually prompt their classmates to do the same as they share powerful uses of language in their discussions.

Regardless of the prompts you ultimately include on the bookmark, make sure they are open-ended enough to allow a range of responses. At least initially, you may want to require students to respond to one or two specific prompts and allow them to choose others on their own. Students tend to consult the prompts often at the beginning of a CDS, then refer to them less frequently as they internalize the questions and become more adept at engaging in civil discourse independently. By reviewing their dailies, you can quickly determine whether students are getting too comfortable with certain prompts and guide them toward others that will push their thinking in different ways.

Dailies

As you'll recall from Chapter 4, dailies are the all-in-one tool students use to prepare for and reflect on their small-group discussions (see Appendices B-2 and B-3). Dailies allow students to keep track of their sticky notes and responses to them, identify the most important topics in their book club discussion, reflect on their participation, and plan ahead for subsequent discussions.

Before discussion, students choose a few sticky notes (usually no more than three) they'd most like to explore, record the page numbers before removing them from the book, and stick them to the left panel. In the right panel they write about why these sticky notes were most important. This panel also directs students to return to the bookmark prompts if they realize the passages they've marked with sticky notes are important but aren't sure how to respond.

Rehearsing ideas in writing beforehand ensures that everyone comes prepared with something to contribute (a double bonus for English Language Learners still working on verbal fluency [Danling Fu 2009]), but you'll need to decide whether you want your students to respond to sticky notes during or outside class. Your students' discussion styles, their work habits outside class, and the length of your class periods should inform your decision. When students write about their sticky notes during class just before a discussion, they can jump in right away because their responses are fresh in their minds. On the other hand, writing about sticky notes outside class gives students time to develop fuller, often more thoughtful responses. Cam likes the immediacy the in-class option provides. Beth uses this option as well, because it guarantees that her students will complete their work. Rebecca, however, relies on her pre-AP tenth graders to complete dailies outside class; they use every precious moment of the fifty-minute class period for discussion.

During discussion, students use the individual responses they've recorded on their dailies to guide their interaction. Because it's unlikely that students will have time to discuss each individual sticky note, they should prioritize the topics that are most important. Cam asks his students to rank their sticky notes before convening for discussion.

After discussion, students complete the metatalk sections of dailies that begin at the bottom of side one and continue on side two. These sections require students to (1) summarize the controversial topics their group discussed, (2) reflect on how well their group engaged in civil discourse, and (3) describe what they can do to ensure an effective discussion the next time their group meets. Students can set norms, use sticky notes, and discuss tough texts, but *unless we ask them to reflect on their processes in writing* they may not understand the importance of what they're doing. We need to explain that the metatalk section of dailies is perhaps the most important because it helps them "talk about their talk."

Let's return for a moment to knowledge transfer because it's essential to understanding why metatalk is so important. Remember that according to Haskell (2000), transfer can occur only if students have command of the knowledge we want them to transfer, a theoretical understanding of why they're transferring it, and lots of practice applying the knowledge in a classroom that encourages them to think beyond an isolated instance of learning.

"Talking about talk" calls to mind the *what,* Haskell's knowledge piece. Knowing the civil discourse strategies they have at their disposal prompts students to reflect on whether they have used these strategies in a particular discussion. The metatalk sections of dailies also remind them why civil discourse is essential for negotiating the troubled waters that inevitably swirl around culturally sensitive topics (that is, Haskell's "theoretical understanding" criterion). In addition, metatalk helps students see the relevance of their interactions. By understanding the cause-and-effect relationship between what gets said and how it gets heard in their small groups, students learn to frame their discourse accordingly (Haskell's "classroom culture" criterion). Finally, metatalk allows students to apply their civil discourse strategies over time through extended discussion of a tough text that contains issues of relevance to their lives as well as the culture at the large (Haskell's "practice" criterion).

Evaluate how successfully students are transferring what they are learning about civil discourse by collecting and assessing their dailies after every discussion.

The Checkpoint Scoring Guide in Appendix A-4 is a helpful and time-efficient assessment tool. (Remember, dailies, like quickwrites, should be viewed as first-draft finals.) Pay special attention to the metatalk sections and address any collective or group-specific concerns.

If you see disparities among group members' descriptions of their experiences, you might have the group discuss the situation. Why do some students feel the discussion is going well while others aren't so sure? How well are they adhering to their group norms? What can they do differently as a group to make the experience more productive for everyone? Based on your observations of their discussions, you should be able to tell whether students need you to mediate this conversation or whether they can handle it independently.

Redistribute dailies before the students' next small-group meeting so students can remind themselves of any resolutions they made. After seeing your responses, students should return dailies to you so that you can attach them to their discussion records (see below); they'll then be able to refer to them as they complete their final projects.

Documenting Discussions: Discussion Records

Anyone who's ever played the telephone game realizes how ephemeral verbal interactions can be. Discussion records (see the example in Figure 5.3) document students' conversations for their future reference and your immediate review. Even though the form is straightforward, it's important to walk through it with students the first time they use it so they understand the purpose of each component. The illustrations below are from a discussion record of a group of Cam's students reading *Gathering Blue*, by Lois Lowry (2000).

The top section of the discussion record calls for basic information and requires groups to select a discussion leader and a scribe. Students should rotate these roles to ensure that every group member gets to practice these valuable skills. The next two sections—Main Ideas Generated from Dailies, and Today's Real Question—function much like minutes taken at a meeting in that the scribe records each student's most valuable contribution to the discussion. This requirement prompts even the most reticent students to participate and requires the entire group to consider their ideas. The phrase "most significant ideas" pushes groups to make decisions about which ideas they want to remember later. You should emphasize that determining the most important ideas is a group decision, not one the scribe makes alone. The *Gathering Blue* group from

Date: _____ Book title: _____ Group name: _____

Group discussion leader: _____ Scribe: _____

(Please choose a different person for each session.)   (Please choose a different person for each session.)

Other group members present: _____

Group members absent: _____

Main Ideas Generated from Dailies. Please write a one-sentence summary of the most significant ideas or questions contributed by each book club member. Write the group member's name beside her/his idea or question.

1. _____

2. _____

3. _____

4. _____

5. _____

6. _____

Today's Real Question:

Consider what lies ahead for your protagonist in the next part of the book. If your protagonist opened a fortune cookie, what do you think it might say?

Your Conclusions:

Figure 5.3 - Book Club Discussion Record

Cam's class recorded these observations and questions as group members' most important contributions during a single discussion:

1. I like how she says "In the beginning."

2. Why was the blue breathing?

3. What's a goldenrod and a goldwood?

When to record their main ideas from the discussion is largely a matter of group preference. Some groups like to record ideas during discussion before they fade away, while others prefer to reflect on the conversation at the end and decide which ideas are most worthy of a permanent record. Either way, the process develops useful skills that students can transfer to other texts because it requires them to report, respond, and reduce. That is, each individual's "report" from their dailies form prompts group interaction leading to their collective "response" to the text. Summarizing the individual's contribution requires the group to step back and "reduce," or distill, its significance in a single phrase, question, or sentence. Students often have difficulty summarizing, and this section of the discussion record lets them practice doing so with the support of their peers.

A word of caution about the main ideas section: you *don't* want students to fill it out round-robin, taking turns until each person has contributed an idea. This disrupts the free-flowing conversation you want to occur and turns "discussion" into a fill-in-the-blank exercise. Cautioning students against this pattern is usually all it takes to help them avoid it. If you observe groups giving in to temptation, however, insist they complete the discussion record at the conclusion of their conversation.

The final section on the discussion record is Today's Real Question. Each group will create a "real question" (one without a preconceived answer) that all members will consider. Real questions are located at the end of the discussion record in order to (1) draw on students' ideas, and thus encourage student ownership, and (2) provide closure. When time permits, you may also want students to report their responses to the whole class. This gives them a glimpse into other groups' thinking; also, when students are reading different texts in their small groups, they get a preview of those other texts.

In the following excerpt, Cam uses a series of real questions to help students make connections between the topics and characters in *Heaven* and their lives outside school.

Today's Real Questions:

- What is **one** of the tough topics that you talked about in this book club?

- How did the **characters in your book** deal with this topic?

- How have you seen **people outside school** deal with this topic?

- How did **your book club** deal with this topic?

Conclusions:

> The tough topic was the ending because it's emotional and she has no one to love as much as her dad. They were upset and now she [has] nobody really with her. They feel sad and feel like nothing can get them through the problem. We were sad for what happened and they got through it. It happened kind of to some of us. Like Courtney's dad left when her mom was pregnant with her. The same thing happened to Kaycie. [Both girls were members of the group.] It is sad 'cause you feel like they don't care about you as much as your mom.

By basing real questions on your instructional goals, thematic connections between books, or any other common concern you would like students to address, you can push students' thinking beyond questions they may have considered on their own in dailies. You can't be everywhere at once in the classroom—and you wouldn't want to be, because you want students to practice engaging in civil discourse independently. This section allows you—even though you aren't physically present—to provide indirect endoscaffolding by modeling open-ended questions that prompt rich discussion.

Cam's real questions above emphasized the concepts associated with tough talk and tough texts and encourage students to think in terms of transfer, and he used the same questions on all the discussion records for this CDS. If you wish to change the emphasis from discussion to discussion, however, here are some examples of other fruitful questions (the carryover from the prompts on the sticky-notes bookmark is intentional, and other prompts on the bookmark make good real questions, too):

- Theme is a statement about life that an author makes through a piece of literature. What are at least three important themes (or statements about life) that your author makes throughout your book?

- So far, how have your overall impressions of the book and the issues it raises been influenced by your own personal experiences and background (in other words, your gender, race, class, and so forth)? Do you think this book is *only* for people who have had certain experiences or are from a certain background? Why or why not?

- The word *conflict* comes from a Latin word that means *to strike together*. What are the forces that are striking together in your protagonist's (main character's) life at this point? Are these conflicts internal, external, or both?

- Why did the author tell this story? What are we the readers to learn, think, or feel after reading this book? What does each person in your group think and why?

- Would you give this book a thumbs-up, a thumbs-down, or something in between? Why?

- What were your best book club discussions about? Why were these discussions the best?

As I mentioned earlier, after each discussion you should staple students' dailies to the back of their discussion records and hang onto them. By the end of the unit, groups will have a satisfyingly thick chronology of their thinking about the book as well as a reflection of their experiences in engaging in civil discourse. These documents provide rich evidence for their final projects. The records also give you a concise record of students' discussions that you can cross-reference with their individual responses in dailies and your own classroom observations to determine how groups are doing independently and when they need extra support.

Documenting Discussions: Field Notes Journal

Another useful tool for conducting classroom observations is a field notes journal, in which you record objective observations of students' discussions on the left side of the page and reflections on those observations on the right side. In the left column, I strive to be as objective as possible in describing what I see; I also record the time every so often to keep track of how events are unfolding in real time. On the right side, I jot down questions and thoughts that occur to me in relation to these events, either as they are occurring or later after class when I can reflect on them more fully.

Appendix A-5 is a field notes form you can reproduce, attach to a clipboard as you make your observations, and then store in a loose-leaf binder. As an alternative, mimic the form in a journal you carry around during discussions. I use marble composition notebooks. When more than one class is working in book clubs or small groups at the same time, I buy a different color for each class so I can find the right notebook at a glance.

Much the way dailies make students pay attention to the texts they're reading, my field notes journal makes me pay attention to the "text" of the classroom, especially when I have a teacher research question in mind. Beth, Cam, Rebecca, and I don't always keep a field notes journal for general book clubs, but we do for civil discourse book clubs. Because civil discourse occurs so rarely in the world at large, documenting what it looks like in the classroom collects valuable evidence to help us understand and describe civil discourse more clearly. In the process, we've discovered that our questions often interest students, too. Because we've shared our observations and emerging questions about civil discourse with students, they have become more reflective about their learning, especially when they think we've "missed something" or are off-track in our interpretations. Like all teacher research, field notes journals provide rich fodder for understanding social dynamics in the classroom and other questions that emerge from your teaching. We've also relied on them heavily as we've shared the results of our teacher research outside of our classrooms at local colloquia and national conferences. The profession not only needs to hear about civil discourse, it needs more teacher researchers' voices contributing to the professional conversation surrounding the enactment of social justice in the classroom (Cochran-Smith and Lytle 2009).

Most important, however, our field notes have helped us tailor instruction and on-the-spot support to students' needs, especially since we cross-reference them with student work like dailies, discussion records, and final projects. Periodically during a CDS, we skim our field notes in connection with student work, looking for patterns of interaction and written responses that indicate small groups or individuals need extra support. Based on what we find, we can provide endoscaffolding for students in various ways—brief conferences with individuals before or after book clubs, written responses to their work in dailies, or drop-in visits during small-group discussions.

Providing Extra Support for Individuals: Responding to Dailies and Talking with Students One-on-One

The civil discourse endoscaffolding you offer individual students is similar to that you provide in other units of study. Your first line of support is your written response to student work. When students' written reactions to the text are thin (most commonly they'll veer into summary rather than interpretation), a comment on the front side of dailies recommending that they address one or more prompts on the sticky-notes bookmark is often all that's necessary to help them respond more deeply.

Field notes allow you to record when a student needs extra support in small-group interactions. If your hunches are confirmed through the student's dailies or other group members' comments, you can note your concerns in the dailies metatalk sections. These written comments usually include (1) an objective observation, (2) a note of encouragement or explanation, and (3) a question/suggestion/admonition. This powerful combination invites a student to step back, reflect on her or his behavior, and plan ahead for the next discussion. For a reticent student, for example, your comment might read, *I notice that you aren't speaking much in the discussion, and I know your group would enjoy hearing your voice more often. The next time your group meets, why don't you identify at least one sticky note that you can share during the discussion?* Sometimes, more direct comments are necessary. For instance, when Beth noticed that a student was using "hallway language" in his small-group discussion, she quoted his words in her response to his dailies, explained why she and the other students (especially the girls) were likely to find it offensive, and asked him to stop using the term in her class and to consider eliminating it from his speech altogether. The language ceased.

Brief one-on-one conversations before or after class can be just as effective as your written comments on dailies, especially when they follow the 1-2-3 combination above. In these instances, an observation and a question may also be in order. For instance, if you have a hunch that one student is dominating discussion, you might say, *When I'm walking around the room, I often hear your voice, but I've noticed that others in your group aren't participating. What ideas do you have about drawing others into the discussion?* This approach calls the student's attention to the behavior in a nonjudgmental way, allows you to collect more information that should confirm or complicate your hunch, and helps you gear your endoscaffolding to the point of need.

Providing Extra Support for Groups: Drop-In Visits and WebQuests

Although your ultimate goal is to help students discuss tough texts without you, groups sometimes need endoscaffolding; that's where drop-in visits and WebQuests come in. When Rebecca and I first began using civil discourse book clubs in her classroom, we intentionally avoided dropping in on small-group discussions. We reasoned that our presence would disrupt students' interactions so much that we'd override our intent to allow them to engage in tough talk independently. In fact, Rebecca and I made a point of telling students that we would move about the room observing their discussions but wouldn't participate. Even when sticky situations arose, we resisted the urge to intervene, preferring to let the students sort things out on their own.

Until we met Dragon Boy, that is.

Jason, or Dragon Boy as we affectionately refer to him, was a student in Rebecca's class who was in a book club reading *Feed* (Anderson 2004), a dystopian science-fiction novel describing a world where people have been implanted with "feeds" that connect them to the Internet. As we observed Jason in his book club, we quickly discovered that he fit the profile of a "bad boy"—the term Karen Gallas (1997) uses for boys who, though highly intelligent and creative, are intent on disrupting the social order of the classroom. The first time the *Feed* group met, Jason caught our attention. After throwing a pencil at one of his classmates, he grabbed the discussion record from the scribe's hands and made a show of scribbling on the back of it.

Though it was difficult, Rebecca and I honored our hands-off policy, observing instead how the other members in the group would respond to Jason. Their body language and verbal exchanges suggested that they were predictably annoyed, but no one retrieved the discussion record. Hoping her quiet presence might be enough to halt Jason's attempt to derail the group, Rebecca moved nearby just in time to hear Hope, the only girl in the group, say, "Are you done, Jason? You didn't read any of it, did you?" Indeed, Rebecca's field notes show that, after noticing that she was nearby, Jason temporarily shifted gears and said, "We should discuss what we wrote." Productive discussion ensued for only a few minutes, however, before Jason yelled, "I'm missing the point of this story!" The bell rang shortly thereafter, and students packed up and went on to their next class.

Rebecca and I put our heads together. We initially assumed that Hope was right; Jason *was* missing the point, most likely because he hadn't read the book. When we looked at his artwork on the back of the discussion record, however, we saw a group of primitive-looking figures with wires and antennas extending from their bodies. The head of a large dragon labeled with the word *COPS* threatened the figures who were yelling, "Ahh my FEED!" in conversation bubbles above their heads. This was far from a random drawing and in fact depicted a scene from the book when the main characters are attacked through their feeds during a visit to a nightclub on the moon; this incident sets the entire plot in motion. When Rebecca cross-referenced Jason's quickwrites (also complete with dragon drawings), she discovered thoughtful written analysis that further contradicted his physical outbursts during book club. What was going on here?

In my field notes journal I recorded the highlights of our discussion as we puzzled through what Rebecca should do if Jason's behavior recurred. Should she stay the course and allow students to work out their own solutions? Because we didn't want to become the book club police, we decided that if Rebecca asked students to review their norms immediately before their next book club discussion and agree how they might proceed if dissension emerged, future attempts by Dragon Boy to disrupt discussion might be quashed. This intervention proved insufficient; at the next book club meeting Jason seized the position of scribe and bulldozed his way through that discussion as well.

The Dragon Boy episode raised larger questions about the tension between private displays of literary engagement and the public personas of resistance that students like Jason feel obligated to maintain. For these students, the question *how do I read this text?* is ultimately superseded by *how do I want my peers to read me?* The more immediate consideration here, however, is what we as teachers ought to do about it when we encounter Dragon Boys in our own classrooms. How many tries should these students get before we intervene? And what should that intervention look like?

If solutions seem obvious, remember that allowing students to work through altercations like these preserves the "civility" component of civil discourse. This incident helped Rebecca and me understand the necessity of *perpetual* scaffolding to help students sustain it. In the years since Dragon Boy, she, Beth, Cam, and I have arrived at a workable protocol that features the judicious use of the "drop-in" when students need a bit of endoscaffolding.

Depending on the kind of support students need, drop-ins can take different forms. The first is the most common: the quick visit, usually no more than a few minutes. Cam is a master of the quick drop-in, providing just enough support to help students get back on track without his turning into the book club police. Three of the most common reasons he drops in are:

1. *To remind students of procedures.* These drop-ins happen most often at the beginning of a book club cycle when his students are still figuring out how to run independent discussions or learning how the response tools work together. Cam takes a moment to explain how dailies work with discussion records, for example, or reminds students what the scribe's responsibilities are.

2. *To describe students' behavior so they can identify alternative courses of actions.* For instance, when one group appeared to be going through the motions of completing the discussion record, he said, "I notice that you're almost finished with your discussion record even though our book club meetings are just beginning. Most of the other groups haven't even started theirs. Why do you think that is?" After the group looked around the room and noticed how other students were using their dailies to prompt discussion rather than fill out the discussion record round-robin, they were able to correct their approach themselves.

3. *To challenge students to consider other perspectives.* After hearing a group of girls making a series of pronouncements like "boys always have to be right" and "kids whose parents are divorced are angry and beat kids up," Cam asked whether they knew what a stereotype was. He provided a brief definition and gave an example of stereotypes directed toward him because he's of Irish descent. He then asked the girls to consider alternatives to the claims they had just made about the character in the book. He listened briefly before moving on to another group, and the girls considered other possibilities by themselves.

Although Cam isn't shy about telling the pencil-throwers to knock if off, his drop-ins are rarely punitive. Rather, he helps students identify and reflect on their own behavior or thinking and to articulate other possibilities. By doing so, he reinforces students' agency and increases the chances that they will stop, think, and reconsider their actions outside the classroom as well.

Since Dragon Boy, Rebecca has also given herself permission to use drop-ins as necessary. Sometimes her drop-ins resemble Cam's quick in-and-outs, but she's also perfected dropping in and staying awhile. Before students divide into small groups, she explains that she'll sometimes pull up a chair during their discussions so she can get a fuller sense of how their ideas are progressing. Mostly she just listens, but occasionally she'll ask a real question, draw out a shy student ("What do you think, Sean?"), or make an observation so that students will elaborate or draw on the text to support their thinking ("That's interesting; say a little bit more").

Beth occasionally uses longer drop-ins with her students as well, especially those who struggle with basic skills like decoding or recall. One semester, she provided extra support for a small group she knew would have difficulty reading *Sky Bridge* (Pritchett 2005). This group included students who were English language learners, read at low levels, had difficulty completing work outside class because of serious life stressors, or some combination of the above. You may recall from Chapter 3 that *Sky Bridge* is a complex novel that deals frankly with issues that were close to these students' lives, such as teen pregnancy, illegal immigration, and high-risk behavior. Even though they were eager to read the book because of these connections, Beth knew this group would need both academic and emotional support.

Consequently, she dropped in regularly, often for longer periods. Especially at the beginning of the novel, she read aloud with the students. I initially worried that the group would become so dependent on her that they wouldn't be able to function independently, but my concern was unwarranted—partly because Beth didn't turn the read-aloud into an exercise in correct pronunciation. Since struggling readers benefit from hearing accomplished readers read with expression, she read, but she also invited them to take turns if they felt comfortable doing so.

Beth's increased level of support with this group was also important because the novel initially emphasizes characterization over plot. Struggling readers often haven't developed the patience and stamina necessary to stick with a text like *Sky Bridge*, especially if the cognitive load they are bearing is considerable (Beers 2002). By reading together as a group early on, Beth and the students shared this load, enabling them to become invested in a text they probably would have abandoned if they had been required to read it entirely on their own. By the time the plot picked up, students were connected to the characters and the challenges and choices they faced. As the unit progressed, the group still began most of the sessions by reading aloud together, but their focus shuttled comfortably between that and discussion of the text.

WebQuests are a more indirect form of endoscaffolding you can provide if the texts students are reading require the kind of contextualization you would routinely provide when an entire class is reading the same book. According to webquest.org, a WebQuest is "an inquiry-oriented lesson format in which most or all the information that learners work with comes from the web." While WebQuests aren't absolutely essential to reading tough texts successfully, they can enhance students' reading experience, particularly when they direct students to links to websites with information about historical context, key allusions, background on the author, or other details key to understanding the plot or controversial aspects of the book. Many publishers also have websites that include video or audio interviews that can really make the author come to life for students.

The key term in the webquest.org definition is *inquiry-oriented*. If you're tempted to save time by simply downloading WebQuests on a book, consider that many of them are just virtual worksheets requiring little or no processing of information. If students are filling in blanks with predetermined answers, why not provide the information on a handout and save them the trouble of an elaborate virtual scavenger hunt? Custom-designed WebQuests, on the other hand, prompt inquiry by directing students to helpful websites with real questions or similarly authentic tasks in mind. Like those on discussion records, the real questions you develop for WebQuests should be discussable as opposed to merely discoverable.

To clarify the differences, consider the following tasks:

> *Prompt 1:* Visit Philip Pullman's official website. Where was Philip Pullman born? How many books has he written?
>
> *Prompt 2:* Take a look at the March 17, 2000, interview with Philip Pullman on this website: www.kidsreads.com/authors/au-pullman -philip.asp. What do you make of his habits as a writer and his views on the process of writing? What are your overall impressions of the author after reading this interview?

The questions in prompt 1 are discoverable: they require students to collect and record information that, while useful, requires no further processing. The questions posed in prompt 2, however, require higher-order thinking: students must both discover and interpret the information they find about Pullman's habits as a writer. In other words, they must arrive at an impression that is discussable with others. A sample WebQuest on *In the Time of the Butterflies* is available at http://fp.seattleschools.org/fpclass/web49/. In it you'll see that discussion is the point.

WebQuests contain three components—a goal, instructions, and a list of the websites the group members will divvy up. Rather than looking up all the sites and answering every question, each student is responsible for making a bulleted list of important information to share with the group in response to her or his assigned site. The next time the group meets to discuss their book, the real question on the discussion record directs them to share their information:

> Take a look at the bulleted list you recorded on your WebQuest. What are a couple of important items you'd like to discuss? Put a star beside them and talk about them with your group.

Making the WebQuest a collective endeavor reinforces the notion that students are constructing knowledge together and also prevents the task from becoming tedious for individuals and repetitive for the group.

Although your instinct may be to assign WebQuests before students begin reading, Rebecca and I have discovered that students are more curious about the information they're looking for after they've had the chance to settle in to the book. We recommend assigning WebQuests after students are invested in the plot, the author's style, and the key subjects in the book, usually just before their second discussion.

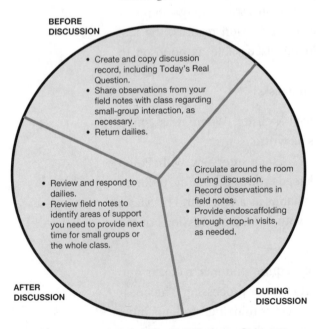

BEFORE DISCUSSION
- Create and copy discussion record, including Today's Real Question.
- Share observations from your field notes with class regarding small-group interaction, as necessary.
- Return dailies.

DURING DISCUSSION
- Circulate around the room during discussion.
- Record observations in field notes.
- Provide endoscaffolding through drop-in visits, as needed.

AFTER DISCUSSION
- Review and respond to dailies.
- Review field notes to identify areas of support you need to provide next time for small groups or the whole class.

Figure 5.4 - Teacher's Role in the Civil Discourse Sequence

When Is It Okay to Be the Teacher?

This chapter describes a host of tools you and your students can use to sustain independent talk about tough texts: norming sheets, sticky-notes bookmarks, dailies, discussion records, field notes, drop-ins, and WebQuests. How all these tools fit together and the respective roles of you and your students are shown in Figures 5.4 and 5.5.

I have a concern about my role as a teacher that may be nagging at the back of your mind as well. I am so committed to student-centered teaching that I've sometimes felt conflicted about "being the teacher" in my own classroom, especially during writing workshop or class discussion. This tension is part of a larger disagreement within our profession among those who have argued for teacher-centered instruction and those who have insisted on classrooms that are practically teacherless. I've come to believe that we should try to balance our approach along a continuum between direct instruction and more subtle support as dictated by student need. In a CDS, you may feel this tension as you circulate during small-group discussions, wondering just how much endoscaffolding is optimal and how much is intrusive. This

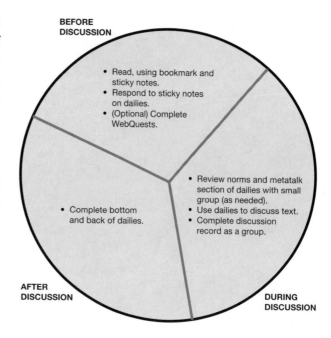

Figure 5.5 - Student's Role in a Civil Discourse Sequence

is normal, I think, because a teacher's presence among students inevitably changes their interactions to some extent. But I also think it's healthy. I don't ever want to let go of that tension, because it helps me pay attention to students' needs and allows me to gear my support to them accordingly until they can function independently of my presence.

Rebecca and I learned from Dragon Boy that it's not only okay but sometimes *necessary* to be the teacher, in the traditional sense of the word. As you determine what level of support to provide for students during a CDS, think of endoscaffolding as the "nudge factor" that can help students successfully carry out a complex process. Stop, look, and listen before intervening; trust your instincts, as bolstered by the body of evidence you've collected in dailies, discussion records, and field notes; then give yourself permission to hang on to the bicycle seat every now and again, never losing sight of your goal to send students out on the open road by themselves.

Chapter 6

So the coin of the realm is not memorizing the facts that they're going to need to know for the rest of their lives; the coin of the realm will be do you know how to find information? Do you know how to validate it? Do you know how to synthesize it? Do you know how to leverage it? Do you know how to communicate it? Do you know how to collaborate with it? Do you know how to problem-solve with it? That's the new twenty-first-century set of literacies, and it looks a lot different than most of us were raised under.

—KEN KAY, PAST PRESIDENT OF THE PARTNERSHIP FOR 21ST CENTURY SKILLS

My son Austen's final eighth-grade project on *The Outsiders* (Hinton 1967), a book he loved well enough to admit it, was the inspiration for this chapter, though not in ways you'd expect. During the time he was reading it, he initiated dinner-table conversations, especially at crucial points in the book: when Ponyboy talks with Cherry at the drive-in, when Ponyboy and Johnny save the children from the burning church, and when Dally is shot. Austen was troubled by the divisions between the Greasers and the Socs and impressed by Ponyboy's bravery. He wondered aloud why Dally committed the robbery that provoked his own death and worried about Ponyboy's concussion, especially since my nephew, who is my son's age, was recovering from brain surgery at the time after being hit by a car. Since the book was inspired by S. E. Hinton's high school experiences, Austen also wanted to know if Tulsa, a city near the area where many of our relatives live, really had gangs of Greasers and, and if so, why did the Socs treat them so badly? Although he hadn't seen the movie at the

Assessing Civil Discourse
Using Twenty-First-Century Skills to Leave No Text Behind

time, he also wanted to know which actors were cast in which roles so he could judge the appropriateness of director Francis Ford Coppola's choices. He was especially fascinated by my husband Will's inside knowledge on this score since Will had auditioned for Coppola when he was still planning to cast unknowns in the film. Finally, Austen loved hearing about how his grandpa's car club had supplied the vintage automobiles used in the scene at the drive-in theater for the fee of one hundred dollars a night per vehicle (two hundred if you also agreed to sit in it all night as an extra).

In other words, Austen had gone far beyond basic plot comprehension (although he'd done this, too). Unbeknownst to him, he had independently demonstrated five of Wiggins and McTighe's (2005) six facets of understanding in that he was able to

- Explain the big ideas of the novel

- Interpret characters' motivations

- Apply his knowledge by speculating about directorial casting decisions

- Reimagine the setting from the author's perspective

- Empathize with the characters' struggles to survive in a class-divided society

Only *self-knowledge*, the sixth facet of understanding, remained, and I, his English-teacher mother, was eager to see how it would manifest itself the weekend he completed his final project.

Would his project reflect what Ken Kay calls the "new coin of the realm?" Would he revisit the text not to regurgitate facts about the novel but to validate, synthesize, and communicate the wealth of information he had learned? Would he have the option to collaborate? Would the project require him to apply twenty-first-century literacy skills to solve new interpretive problems?

After a twenty-dollar trip to the craft store and three hours' work, Austen had written a one-page biography of Darry, Ponyboy's older brother (chosen, even though he was only mentioned in passing, because "Darry would be easy to do the project on"), and had created a "Darry doll" so unsightly that he carried it to school the next day in a paper bag (see Figure 6.1).

An opportunity ripe for authentic assessment of Austen's knowledge about an assigned book he had truly loved had passed unrealized, in my mind a case of multiple intelligences theory gone bad. Although the Darry doll technically met all the requirements listed on the rubric, his teacher would have little insight into Austen's deep engagement with *The Outsiders* when she assessed his work. More distressing to me as a parent, however, was that the three hours he spent completing the project had neither extended his already rich understanding of the text nor compelled him to reflect on the implications of his reading experiences for his own life in a society in which inequity still exists.

In fairness to Austen's teacher, who was implementing the district-mandated curriculum, doll making was only one of the

Figure 6.1 - Darry Doll

options offered as a final project. Book jackets, newspapers, and billboards that summarized the book's main events were other possibilities. Students could also write about the literary elements Hinton used in the novel. In exasperation, I asked Austen why he hadn't chosen to write an essay. "No one ever chooses that one," he explained. "I am *not* getting up in front of the class to talk about 'literacy elements' or whatever they're called. Seriously, Mom."

Seriously. The experience made me want to avoid the Darry doll debacle at all cost by making sure that the projects in this chapter will help your students deepen their understanding about tough texts like *The Outsiders*. It's important to me that the text doesn't get left behind. I also want the projects to meet the following characteristics of authentic assessment:

- Be *connected to prior instruction* by representing the cumulative result of prior formative experiences with the concept of civil discourse and the literary texts at hand.

- Be *opportunistic rather than obligatory* by presenting new chances to synthesize knowledge and prompting in students a "continuing impulse to learn" (Oldfather 1993).

- Be *performance-based and in situ* by giving students opportunities to construct and demonstrate knowledge collaboratively *in the midst of* literacy acts rather than to merely recall and report isolated facts from the text after reading it.

- Be *open-ended and multimodal* by allowing students a range of creative options for conveying and reflecting on what they've learned, such as talking, writing, visualizing, and making artifacts.

- Be *instructionally defensible* in that they are based on a recognized body of standards (e.g., NCTE/IRA 1996) and recommendations for twenty-first-century learning (e.g., recommendations issued by the Partnership for 21st Century Skills).

Most important, the projects had to be tested by real students in actual classrooms with fantastic results. The five projects in this chapter have all these characteristics.

The twenty-first-century skills Ken Kay points to in the quotation that opens this chapter bear little resemblance to the skills many adults used when they were in school. How do we design authentic assessments *and* allow students to draw on and further develop twenty-first-century skills that we ourselves may find unfamiliar? The projects below let you assess students' understanding of literature in ways that will allow them to practice civil discourse *and* employ twenty-first-century skills at the same time. None of these projects leave the text behind: students must revisit the book they've read and the dailies they've written, synthesizing their prior interpretations and civil discourse processes to create something new.

The discussions below provide the origin, description, and rationale for each project. Reproducible handouts and scoring guides for these assignments are available at www.heinemann.com/toughtalk when you click on the companion resources tab. In addition, the participation statements in Figures 6.2 and 6.3 can be adapted for each group project. Together, students complete a group participation statement (Figure 6.2) that lists each member's role in creating the project and states the grade that group members think they should receive. Students also complete individual participation statements (Figure 6.3) that allow them to agree or disagree with the group participation statement, state what they believe their individual grade should be, and briefly explain why.

At the top of the group participation statement, students must document the division of labor, making each individual's contributions to the project apparent for all to see. The bottom of the statement requires the group to review the scoring guide before evaluating the quality and completeness of their work. This prompts one last look at the final product; if something is missing, students can't say they were uninformed.

The individual participation statement prevents "groupthink." Students say whether they agree or disagree with the group participation statement (and why) and can communicate anything else they want you to know about their individual contributions. It's not a tattling mechanism per se but does prevent less conscientious students from coasting by on other students' hard work. Looking at the group and individual participation statements you can easily note any discrepancies in the division of labor. If and when these appear, you can follow up.

Mandala and Found Poem

Mandalas are circular designs used by ancient cultures to symbolize the universe, totality, or wholeness through concentric geometric forms and other images. They can take many forms, from enormous sand drawings made by Buddhist monks as a form of meditation to life-size mazes to illustrated designs. I adapted mandalas for my AP-English students after Cindy Cotner asked my teacher research group to use various media—watercolors, colored pencils, pastels, and such—to create a mandala representing the "world" encompassed by our teacher research studies. To be honest, I approached the exercise with trepidation because I'm more comfortable expressing myself in writing, but combining the visual (the mandala) with the verbal (our subsequent discussion about our representations) challenged me to think about my work in ways that either process would not have accomplished alone. Other

Figure 6.2 - Group Participation Statement

Book	*Looking for Alaska*

Group Member's Name	Role in Creating Project	Role in Presentation
Antonio	Suggested ideas from my dailies and drew part of the Janus mask	Explained the symbols I drew and talked about what the colors mean
Tania	Suggested ideas from my dailies and found the quotations for the mask	Read the quotations and explained why we chose them
Molly	Looked back at all the group discussion records to come up with ideas for important events and decisions Pudge made; helped draw	Talked about the symbols we used for important events
Marcus	Suggested ideas from my dailies and drew the symbols to represent Pudge's public self	Explained the symbols I drew
Elena	Was group leader and used everybody's ideas to write the poem on the mask	Read the poem and explained where we put symbols on the mask
Chris	Suggested ideas from my dailies and drew the symbols to represent Pudge's private self	Explained the symbols I drew

After reviewing the scoring guide, we believe that our group should receive a grade of <u>A–</u>, *and here's why:*

We all worked really hard on our mask, and we think it looks good. We all worked together to come up with ideas and made sure that we met all the requirements on the handout you gave us. Everyone presented their part of the mask, and we were prepared to answer questions. We could have used a few more symbols.

Signatures _____

Figure 6.3 - Individual Participation Statements

Name   Antonio

I (agree)/disagree (circle one) with the information on the group participation statement, and here's why:

I agree with what it says on our group statement. We all gave our ideas. Elena was a good leader.

After reviewing the scoring guide, I believe that I should receive a grade of <u>A-</u>, and here's why:

I did my part and was ready for the presentation. I maybe could have added more symbols.

- -

Name   Tania

I (agree)/disagree (circle one) with the information on the group participation statement, and here's why:

I agree with the group statement. We all worked hard and finished our parts.

After reviewing the scoring guide, I believe that I should receive a grade of <u>A-</u>, and here's why:

Even though we might have found more symbols, I looked at everybody's dailies and listened to their ideas about the quotes so we could choose the best ones.

- -

Name   Molly

I agree/disagree (circle one) with the information on the group participation statement, and here's why:

I mostly agree with the group statement. Some of the people in our group weren't always paying attention.

After reviewing the scoring guide, I believe that I should receive a grade of <u>A</u>, and here's why:

I had to review all of the discussion records to come up with ideas. I drew my symbols and helped with the other ones. I also helped Elena make sure we met all of the requirements.

- -

Name   Marcus

I (agree)/disagree (circle one) with the information on the group participation statement, and here's why:

I agree with what we wrote on the group statement. We were confused about some parts at first, but we got it figured out.

After reviewing the scoring guide, I believe that I should receive a grade of <u>A-</u>, and here's why:

Sometimes me and Tania got a little distracted, but I got my part done.

---

members of my teacher research group have used mandalas to great effect with fifth graders, community college students, graduate students, faculty members, and even attendees at the International Conference of Teacher Research (see O'Donnell-Allen 2005).

My AP students were reading *Narrative of the Life of Frederick Douglass* at the time, and I thought the mandala would be an ideal way to help them represent the "world" of this tough text. Creating a mandala in a small group would allow them to construct new meaning in collaboration with their peers by:

- Reviewing the text to determine its central players, their relationships, and the key themes and controversies.

- Considering the text holistically and representing their interpretations visually through a unified system of images.

- Reflecting on their experiences by way of civil discourse.

The assignment sheet, planning guide, and scoring guide for the mandala project are available at www.heinemann.com/toughtalk. Please click on the companion resources tab to access the forms.

Despite the evidence students had provided in their journals and discussions that they understood the landscape of *Narrative*, zooming in on Douglass's language posed a greater challenge. I knew they also needed individual practice in close reading, especially because style analysis is a key skill students must demonstrate on the AP exam. To make the text and the analytical process more accessible and to add a measure of individual accountability, I supplemented the mandala assignment by asking students to create a "found poem" from a passage of *Narrative* that they considered significant to the work as a whole.

Most often, writers create found poems by selecting words from another piece of writing (an article, a menu, and so forth) and putting them back together again in poetic form (Tsujimoto 1988). But I felt the technique poets refer to as "erasure"—that is, blacking out words and phrases from photocopied pages of texts until a poem emerges from those that remain—would help my students analyze Douglass's diction, imagery, figurative language, and organization more closely. To complete their found poems, students had to:

- Revisit the text to select a significant passage.

- Read the passage closely to glean its meaning.

- Analyze style by eliminating the words and phrases they deemed insignificant in conveying Douglass' meaning.

- Use the remaining words as raw materials for creating a new text (i.e., the found poem) that conveyed their understanding of the original passage.

Visit www.heinemannn.com/toughtalk and click on the companion resources tab to access an assignment sheet and scoring guide for the found poem.

To add yet another layer of interpretation to these tasks, I first asked groups to present their mandalas to the class and entertain questions from their peers. Then they read their poems aloud and posted them on the walls of our classroom. Next, they took a "gallery walk," viewing the found poems and using sticky notes to comment on them. We ended with a class discussion on the stylistic and thematic patterns students noticed among the poems. Taken together, the mandala, found poem, presentations, gallery walk, and closing discussion gave students multiple entry points into the book.

In my class, we used *Narrative* as a common text that we discussed both as a whole class and in small groups, but the sequence worked equally well when Rebecca used it with her pre-AP sophomores in book clubs. Figure 6.4 is a mandala one book club created for *The Golden Compass*.

Figure 6.4 - Mandala for *The Golden Compass*

The Map Project and Travel Guide

The map project originated when Rebecca was focusing primarily on the structural elements of texts (plot, character, setting, theme, and so on). It resembles the mandala project in that both are visual interpretations that students create in small groups, but the projects differ in important ways. The mandala project asks students to approach a text holistically—to see it as an entire world, much as one would take a satellite view of earth from space. The map project, on the other hand, requires students to view the text more analytically, to move in closer and examine its structural features, much as one would use Google Maps to zoom in on a particular area of the Earth to see actual streets, houses, football arenas, and rivers. High school and middle school map project assignment sheets, planning guides, and scoring guides are available at www.heinemann.com/toughtalk when you click on the companion resources tab.

The maps created resemble the cartoonish, not-to-scale promotional maps vacation destinations often use to highlight points of interest like landmarks, local attractions, and restaurants. The textual points of interest students identify in their maps are metaphorical parallels—*landmarks* could refer to important settings, *monuments* could mark key characters and events, and *road signs* could mark points of conflict. Students use icons to represent these textual points of interest and provide a legend at the bottom of the map. The assignment sheets on the website (www.heinemann.com/toughtalk) provide several prompts for these icons, but these are my favorites:

> *Xs and Arrows*—On pirate maps, X usually marks the spot where buried treasure lies. On maps of campuses, malls, and airports, red arrows often indicate, "You are here." What treasures are to be found in this book? Where are they located? Where would you locate yourselves in the territory of this book?
>
> *Uncharted Territory*—Hundreds of years ago when English mapmakers wanted to indicate the limits of the known world on a map, they would write "Beyond this place, there be dragons." What subjects, issues, and questions remained unresolved in your book club discussions? How did this book make you think? What questions are you asking now that you weren't before you read this book?

These prompts push students to revisit the most controversial issues they have addressed in their discussions of the book and consider where they stand, personally and as a group, in relation to these issues. This is evident in the map in Figure 6.5 that Rebecca's students created after reading *Postcards from No Man's Land* (Chambers 1999), a novel with parallel story lines.

The four lines traveling up the center of the map represent the pathways the students identified while reading the book. The path on the far left represents Geertrui's story line. Geertrui is significant both because she wants to be released from her terminal illness by euthanasia and because of her relationship with the grandmother of the other main character. The second path is the author's. The third path represents the students' own journey through the book, and the path on the far right belongs to sixteen-year-old Jacob, the lead character in the other story line who travels to Amsterdam to honor his grandfather's service in WWII. While in Amsterdam, Jacob learns the truth about his grandfather's relationship with Geertrui and develops

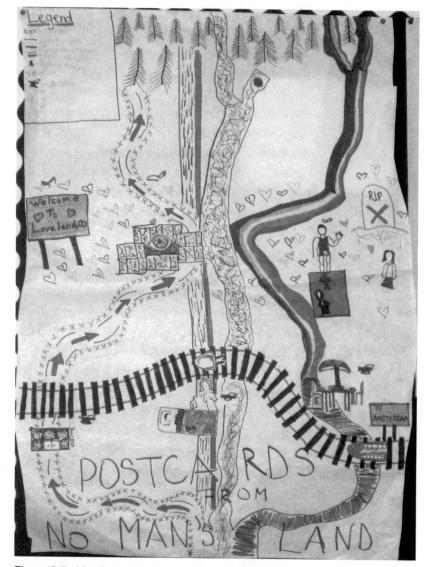

Figure 6.5 - Map Project for *Postcards from No Man's Land*

relationships with new friends who cause him to question his gender identity; thus students colored the bottom third of Jacob's path blue to indicate setting (i.e., Amsterdam's canals) and chose a multicolored rainbow design to represent sexual diversity.

The four paths start out together at the bottom of the map, separate as the stories progress, meet again in the middle, and diverge once more at the top. During their presentation, students explained that the pathways on their map represented a chronology. Students "joined" Geertrui and Jacob's stories when they began reading the text. Their paths separated as the two story lines developed, then merged again as students discovered how the story lines related to one another. All the paths on their map divide again and end up in "uncharted territory." Students depicted uncharted territory as a forest at the top of the map to represent the choices Geertrui, the author, the students, and Jacob are faced with by the novel's end. Geertrui's uncharted territory was the choice she must make about whether to end her life. Jacob's uncharted territory was his decision about whether to tell his grandmother Sarah about his grandfather's relationship with Geertrui or to keep it a secret.

The students' explanation of their own uncharted territory was the most interesting. The dot at the top right of their path before it splits and heads into the forest marks the place where their literal relationship with the book ends when they turned the final page. During their presentation, Rebecca asked students what happened to their road. If they had finished the book, why did it split and continue on into uncharted territory? Her students explained that the book provided "a different outlook from what we were used to," a new way of looking at the world that remained "uncharted like the book."

The *Postcards* group's map contains many other points of interest not described here, but this discussion of the pathways demonstrates how the map project allows students to focus on the structural aspects of the text—parallel story lines, character development, conflict, and key controversial issues like euthanasia and gender identity—while at the same time reflecting on their own journeys through the text.

Student presentations are an integral element of these projects, not add-ons. When students create visual interpretations like mandalas, maps, or body biographies, they gain new understanding of the text as they explain their interpretive choices to the class (Smagorinsky and O'Donnell-Allen 1998). At least at first, you may have to prompt students to do more than just point and describe the symbols on their map, as Rebecca did with the *Postcards* group. If Rebecca hadn't asked the simple question "What happened to your road?," neither she nor the rest of her class would have heard how a novel like *Postcards from No Man's Land* can extend students' journeys beyond the last page of a book to a new way of looking at the world. Don't hesitate to use your questions as scaffolds to help students explain the symbolic import of the symbols they've drawn; you want to get at the reasons underlying students' interpretive choices.

You also gain insight into students' individual experiences with a text by assigning travel guides to accompany the group maps. Like the found poem assignment described in the previous section, the travel guides provide a measure of individual accountability. But rather than focusing tightly on the language of the text as the found poem requires, the travel guide gives students a place to review the book and walk the reader through their individual experiences of it. If you're using a book club approach to tough texts, the travel guides have an audience that automatically extends beyond the teacher to the students in the class who haven't yet read the book.

Also available when you go to the website www.heinemann.com/toughtalk and click on the companion resources tab: A middle school travel guide assignment which balances prompts students are required to address (book blurb, author blurb, book review, and book club review) and offers several from which they can choose. An accompanying planning sheet gives students space to record ideas for content and presentation, and a scoring guide is also provided.

Janus Project, Mind Map, and Life Letter

The Janus project is an adaptation of the body biography (O'Donnell-Allen 2006). Janus, commonly depicted with two faces, is the Roman god of gates and doors, beginnings and endings, and important transitions in life, such as moving from childhood to adulthood. I named this project after Janus because we all have two sides—the side others see and the one no one but ourselves sees. For this project, which was created to help Beth's high school students develop their character analysis skills at the completion of a mythology unit, groups select a character from their tough text and create a two-sided mask depicting the *public* self the character projects to others and the *private* self the students perceive the character to be.

Creating the Janus mask, like the mandala and the map, requires students to return to the text and their dailies to find ideas for the symbols they'll draw to represent their interpretations. The difference is that this project focuses heavily on character. Even when the symbols refer to events in the book, these events draw their importance from choices and changes the characters make. Students must also include the three most important lines from the book by or about the character and an original text written about the character or from her or his perspective (texts students have produced include poems, letters, and diary entries). The assignment sheet and scoring guide for this project are available at www.heine-mann.com/toughtalk when you click on the companion resources tab.

Figure 6.6 is a Janus mask Beth's students created for Tasha, the teenage mother in *Imani All Mine*. A sun on Tasha's forehead represents her daughter Imani's birth and unites both sides of the mask. The question mark in the sun suggests Tasha's initial uncertainties about motherhood. The right side of the mask depicts Tasha's public self. The red *F* at the top symbolizes her English teacher's fixed opinion of Tasha as a lazy student and refers specifically to the *F* he gave her when she was unable to attend school, even though she had made up all her work. Students chose a quotation capturing Tasha as a mother who rocks her daughter Imani in "arms strong like the branches of a tree," making the baby feel "safe because I'm holding her and won't ever let her fall." Clockwise from the quotation, a red dress is used to show that most of the characters, including her own mother, viewed Tasha as promiscuous, even though her pregnancy was the result of rape. The extinguished

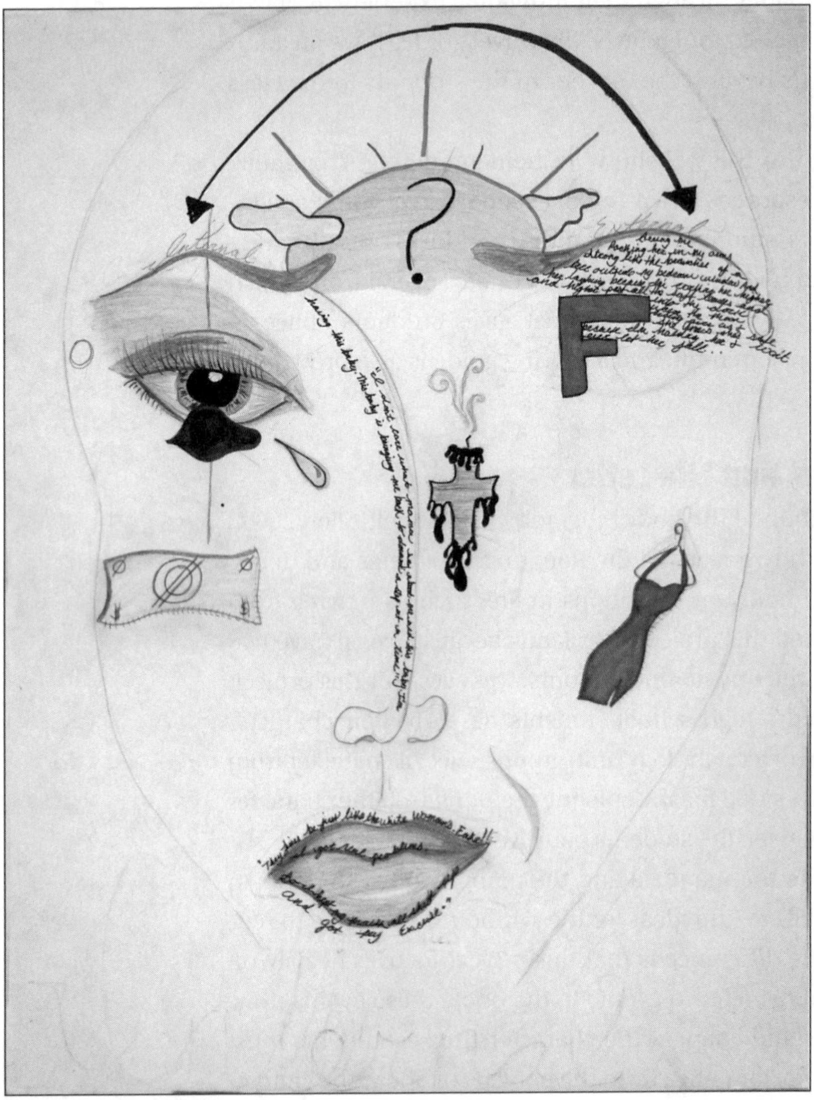

Figure 6.6 - Janus Mask of Tasha

grey candle in the shape of a cross next to the nose represents Tasha's loss of faith after Imani is killed during a drive-by shooting.

Like the sun on her forehead, Tasha's closed mouth unites both sides of the mask. Students lined the lips with a quotation that reveals the discrepancy between the way others see Tasha and the way she sees herself. "I got real problems," Tasha says, yet she keeps her mouth "all shut up" because she knows it would do no good to share them with others who assume the worst about her.

The left side of the mask depicts Tasha's private self. The dollar bill on her cheek has zeroes on it to emphasize her poverty, and the tear falling from her bloodshot eye symbolizes Imani's death. Students colored the freeform shape below the iris purple to represent Tasha's bravery in the face of tragedy. Likewise, the quotation down the bridge of her nose illustrates Tasha's stubborn will to survive, even though she becomes pregnant again by the end of the book, this time with her boyfriend's baby: "I don't care what Mama say about me and this baby. I'm having this baby. This baby is bringing me back to Imani a step at a time."

Although products like this Janus mask are an impressive display of collaborative interpretation, Beth also needs to make sure the wide range of students in her classes can analyze texts individually. Some are voracious independent readers, but many have spotty skills, having fallen through the cracks in mainstream schools. That's why Beth also asks each student to create a mind map and life letter prior to completing the Janus project. The mind map helps students begin thinking in symbolic terms about the text and is both a prewriting activity for the life letter and a "previsualizing" activity for the Janus mask. The life letter requires students to translate the visual symbols from their mind map into words—to describe how well the book related to their own life as they got to know the main character—and to reflect on how well they participated in their civil discourse book club. Combining visual and verbal activities helps Beth's students think more deeply about literary texts. The mind map/life letter assignment sheet and scoring guide are provided at www.heinemann.com/toughtalk and suggest several prompts to get their creative juices flowing.

The Podcasting Project

If you're tempted to skip this section because technology just isn't your cup of tea, I urge you to read at least a few more paragraphs. Many teachers are afraid of technology for seemingly valid reasons. "But something may go wrong," they say. (It will.) "I might not know what to do!" (You won't.) "What if I can't answer all the kids' questions?" (You won't be able to.) But haven't you felt the same way about other lessons you've tried for the first time, even when they didn't involve technology?

Even though we shared these same worries, Beth and I swallowed hard and tried the podcasting project with her students. With two computers and very little podcasting experience between us, we survived and the kids *thrived*, willingly revisiting the text they had read in their book clubs, referring back to their dailies, and even putting in extra time outside class to create a product they were proud of. At the conclusion of the project, we realized there was nothing to be afraid of. A little sheepishly, we've been assigning podcasts ever since.

If you have teenagers in your house, you know they routinely use technology to communicate in their lives outside school. Most students today do so voluntarily, early, and often, perhaps more so than any previous generation. More important, most students don't consider the extraordinary number of Facebook entries, emails, blogs, videos, and fan fiction pieces they produce and consume as reading or writing, even though these texts require them to practice sophisticated literacy skills (Pew Internet and American Life Project 2008). Despite their digital prowess, however, students are far less likely to use technology in school for much more than "an add-on, a 'tool' to support forms of practice that are well-rehearsed" like the traditional research paper (Leander 2006, 46; see also Kajder 2007). In other words, they mostly use technology in school to *collect* information rather than to *communicate* or connect (Kirkland 2009). We created the podcast project for Beth's students in part to rectify this disparity.

Beth knew her students would respond well to an invitation to use technology, period, but we also thought the project could:

1. Address more traditional language arts skills like summarizing text and analyzing theme.

2. Help students reflect more formally on their civil discourse processes.

3. Widen the audience for their critical review of the book since their podcasts could be shared with future classes.

The project worked—so well that I recorded the following in my field notes journal:

> What strikes me about this scene is how "normal" it seems for the kids, but I bet innocent bystanders, many local teachers and adminis-

trators, and even members of the profession at large wouldn't believe it could happen in a high school at all, especially in an alternative high school. This is a testament to some combination of the climate and expectations Beth has established in the CDS, the books themselves, and the kids' dedication to reading and participating in book clubs. Otherwise, why would they be reviewing their stickies, rereading their books, and working on this project without complaint?

Actually, I did hear a few "complaints," but they were all reflexive. When trying to figure out how to get music to underlie the podcast in GarageBand, for instance, one girl said more to herself than to any one in particular, "This is definitely not what I wanted to do. It's fun, but I don't know how to make it sound good." Another time, I heard a boy say to a group huddled around the computer, "That just sounds weak. What if we try this?" When was the last time you heard a student say, "Writing this essay is fun but difficult," or make a frank assessment about his work to his classmates before eagerly trying another approach? Yet another compelling reason to try podcasting is students' intense engagement with their work and their willingness to revise it extensively. Like other teachers who have assigned digital writing, Beth and I have found that students care so much about the medium, they're willing to care about the message as well. (For more on students' willingness to revise digital compositions, see Herrington, Hodgson, and Moran 2009 and Hicks 2009.)

That's not to say that Beth's students didn't generate a good bit of print-based writing in conjunction with this project as well. In addition to dailies, students completed daily quickwrites, several drafts of a paragraph analyzing theme, life letters as described in the previous section, and outlines or verbatim scripts for their podcasts. The following quickwrite prompts helped students prepare for their podcasts:

- Describe the setting of your book. How is it important to what's going on in the book?

- What seems to be the conflict thus far in your book? What's going on?

- What controversial issues from you novel might come up in your book club discussion today? How will you handle this if it gets uncomfortable?

- What do you think the author of your book is trying to say to his or her readers? Why write this book?

- Write about anything this book is reminding you of. What connections are you making?

- Get into the mind of your character. Speak to me as Libby, Charlie, or Pudge. Tell me what's on your mind.

- Be a book critic. Rate your book on a scale of 1–10. Would you recommend it to others? Why or why not? Should we use it again as a book choice for book clubs? Why or why not?

From start to finish, this CDS took about five weeks. During the first week, we introduced the concept of civil discourse and students began using response strategies with starter texts and selected their book club books. During weeks 2 and 3, they read their books at the start of class every day, participated in book club discussions, and composed thematic analysis paragraphs and mind maps (the individual components of the unit). In the final two weeks, they met author Laura Pritchett, author of *Sky Bridge* (2005), and created and presented their podcasts and mind maps.

Access to technology can be a challenge. Beth's school did have a lab with PCs, but because of district technology restrictions, she was unable to have a PC-compatible audio recording and editing program installed on the computers, even a free one like Audacity. Our access to technology was thus limited to the two MacBooks we personally owned and three iPods and external microphones we borrowed from the Colorado State University Writing Project. Students worked out a schedule for sharing the equipment. We used GarageBand as the editing program because it is automatically installed on Macs, which also have built-in microphones. Students were also able to record their podcasts as "voice memos" using Tune Talks, affordable microphones that plug into the bottom of iPods and produce high-quality recordings. Students then synced the voice memos to the MacBooks and converted them to MP3 files so they could edit them in GarageBand (see www.heinemann.com/toughtalk and click on the companion resources tab for directions).

If you haven't made a foray into podcasting yet, I know the paragraph above may sound daunting, but as digital natives, the kids were unintimidated. I wrote *NO FEAR* in capital letters in my field notes journal the day they began using the equipment. Before that, though, Beth and I had laid some careful groundwork so that the kids understood our expectations.

We introduced the project by listening to an excerpt from the "Superpowers" episode of *This American Life*, the program produced by Chicago Public Radio and broadcast on National Public Radio. Archived episodes are available on the program's website (www.thisamericanlife.org/) and can be downloaded from iTunes for $0.99. This terrific episode poses three questions:

> Can superheroes be real people? (No.) Can real people become super-heroes? (Maybe.) And which is better: flight or invisibility? (Depends who you ask.)
>
> [www.thisamericanlife.org/search?keys=invisibility]

Like everyone featured in the broadcast, the kids were immediately taken with the questions, writing in their journals and discussing them enthusiastically before we listened to the excerpt. We asked students, as they listened, to jot down what they noticed about how the episode was structured. Though they didn't use these precise terms, the key features they named were commentary from the host, interviews, conversation, music, and ambient (or background) noise. We then listened to the excerpt a second time, this time asking students to make notes about how these features were sequenced. Beth copied the students' observations on the board, and they noticed how some features were separated by distinct breaks, while others faded into the one that followed. Before students moved into their groups to begin planning their own podcasts, Beth reviewed the assignment sheet and pointed out that they had already begun thinking about all the assigned features in their journals and mind maps.

Students spent the next few class periods working on their podcasts. During that time, students listened to another podcast Beth and I and a student in one of Beth's other classes had made about *Imani All Mine* (Porter 2000). We made our own for a couple of reasons: (1) Beth and I wanted to learn how to use the equipment so that we could help students through the process and (2) we wanted students to hear a model recorded by "amateurs" and based on the assignment they were completing themselves.

Handouts related to the podcasting project are available at www.heinemann .com/toughtalk.

- The assignment sheet gives a project overview.

- The various sections of the planning guide help students divvy up roles and plan the *content* of the podcast.

- The podcast sequencing chart helps students map out the *structure* of their podcasts after they've planned the content. It's akin to a storyboard a filmmaker might use, the main difference being that the filmmaker thinks in "shots," while the podcaster thinks in "segments."

- The tech talk handout outlines the basics of GarageBand.

- The scoring guide helps you evaluate their final products but is also a nifty checklist students can use to make sure they've met all the project requirements.

This list of handouts implies a linear process (students will plan the content first, then the structure, and so on), though we realize the composing process is much more recursive. While it is important that they plan group roles first, students move fluidly back and forth in planning, composing, and editing both the content and sequence of their podcasts. (If you remember writing the outline for your own high school research paper *after* you wrote the paper, you understand what I mean.) In other words, the planning guide is truly meant for planning, wherever that step may occur in the composing process. If you don't get too obsessive about these tools, they can help students; but they'll be a pain in the neck if you use them in a lockstep fashion.

The Multiliteracies Project

Traditionally, literacy is defined as the singular ability to read and write print-based texts. In today's world, however, even mundane tasks require us to think of *reading, writing*, and *texts* in broader ways—that is, to use *multiliteracies* (Anstéy and Bull 2006). The multiliteracies project requires students to use several kinds of texts (print, digital, audio, visual) to explore a pressing question they have about reading. The project has four components: an artist statement describing the author's aesthetic intent, the project itself, a reflection, and a bibliography. Students workshop their projects with their peers in class, help design the scoring guide, and display their final products to the class in a gallery walk as a final exam. During the gallery walk, each student stands beside her or his project and entertains any questions viewers might have. Armed with sticky notes, viewers make brief written comments that they post beside the work for the artist to keep.

Students in my classes have created an extraordinary array of multiliteracies projects, including:

- A large map linked to photographs of people around the world whom the student had interviewed about their reading experiences in school

- A survey of students who are deaf and/or blind, a video interview with an American Sign Language interpreter signing and verbally discussing the special needs of this student population, a Braille transcript of the interview, and a brochure of teacher resources for helping deaf and blind students

- A PowerPoint presentation featuring passages from *To Kill a Mockingbird* hyperlinked to contextual information (written and pictorial definitions of vocabulary words, websites with historical information, and so forth)

Since the last example above worked so well with a tough text like *To Kill a Mockingbird*, I decided to adapt the multiliteracies project into a CDS tough text assignment (see Multiliteracies Project Assignment at www.heinemann .com/toughtalk when you click on the companion resources tab). Students Rhonda and Corey used PowerPoint software to create a "book trailer" for *The Perks of Being a Wallflower* (Chbosky 1999). They recruited and cast friends in the roles of the novel's main characters and photographed them at sunrise in the Fort Collins foothills to represent a turning point in the title character Charlie's social and emotional growth. On one slide, the actors clustered together to portray Charlie's gradual transition from wallflower to a member of a peer group. Another image silhouetted Charlie against the rising sun, his arms outstretched to reflect the epiphanic moment in the novel when he "feels infinite" making memories with friends for the first time. Other photographs represented various aspects of Charlie's life—music, school, drugs and alcohol, and the truck he rides around in with one of his friends. Playing beneath these slides was an original song Rhonda and Corey wrote and performed from Charlie's perspective called "You Make Me Feel So Infinite."

Another student, Lisa, used pages from a copy of *The Catcher in the Rye* to create an altered book to serve as a visual representation of Holden Caulfield, whom she considered to be "the classic adolescent." She found a well-worn copy of the book in a used bookstore, carefully tore it apart, and reassembled it in the

Figure 6.7 - *Catcher in the Rye* altered book

form of the hound's-tooth jacket Holden loans to his roommate Stradlater at the beginning of the book (see Figure 6.7).

Although she originally wanted to reconstruct the book in the form of Holden's hunting hat, Lisa ultimately chose the jacket because it was larger and allowed her to use every page of the book. As she explained in her artist statement, the black words on the white pages were reminiscent of the hound's-tooth pattern, and "jackets are easily slipped on and off, just like picking up a book and putting it down. When a reader becomes absorbed in a book, it is said they are 'wrapped up' in it. Wearing this jacket literally allows you to surround yourself in the text." At the gallery walk, Lisa also explained that the jacket had symbolic import, concealing Holden's emotional vulnerability while at the same time marking his desire to enter adulthood.

Lisa told me that in the process of constructing the jacket, she developed a new intimacy with the novel, rereading every page and making the happy discovery that another reader had highlighted and underlined passages and penned observations in the margins of the pages where significant events occurred. This other reader's written transactions prompted a literary kinship of sorts, so much so that Lisa chose to feature the annotated pages prominently on the jacket's pockets and lapel. She transformed the cover of the book into buttons, lapel trim, a label, and an ascot to signify

Holden's socioeconomic privilege and to reemphasize his position on the cusp of adulthood.

Amanda, another student, used Comic Life software to retell Chapter 3 of *The Catcher in the Rye* in the form of a graphic novel. She selected this chapter because she felt it demonstrated Holden's literary interests, his interaction with other adolescents, and his biting sense of humor. In creating her comic, Amanda alternated between linguistic and visual semiotic systems. First she sectioned the chapter into "ministories" and created a storyboard. Next, she scanned in photographs she had taken of a friend she had persuaded to act as Holden and selected other appropriate copyright-free images from Creative Commons on Flickr. She then found significant lines from the chapter to correspond with the images and worked in Comic Life to combine the words and images into a cohesive whole. She used color, shadowing, and frame size to convey the relative importance of images and words.

In the students' artist statements and reflections and in their conversations with me about their multiliteracies projects, four themes emerged:

1. *The project met traditional language arts objectives aimed at literary analysis.* Creating the projects forced students to examine the literary text closely and critically again and again, thus deepening their understanding of the characters, significant events, and primary themes as well as the author's stylistic choices.

2. *Using multiple texts (all of which included print, by the way) wasn't merely a shiny add-on.* Rather, this requirement stretched students' interpretive capacities, pushing them to express what they'd learned in a way that wouldn't have been possible had they used print texts alone. According to Rhonda and Corey, multiliteracies projects "allow students to respond to a text in ways other than simply writing a paper." These projects "force [students] to tap into their creativity, as well as to use their critical thinking skills to . . . convey their understanding of a topic in nontraditional ways."

3. *The project required students to use multiliteracies strategically.* The open-ended nature of the project gave students artistic freedom, which was both rewarding and frustrating. Because of formulaic curriculum and standardized assessments, students sometimes have difficulty dealing with ambiguity. A clear assignment sheet and scoring guide, the suggestions provided on a "choice board," and models from prior

classes alleviated anxiety to some extent, but ultimately students had to use multiliteracies to solve problems, access appropriate resources, make deliberate aesthetic decisions, and reflect on their work.

4. *The social aspect of the project was key.* Workshopping the project with peers, having a say in how they would be assessed by designing the scoring guide as a class, and presenting their work to and getting feedback from multiple audiences (their teacher, peers, and, in some cases, the Internet) increased students' sense of efficacy and motivated them to create a quality product.

Three handouts on the website (www.heinemann.com/toughtalk) are adaptations of my original project. The assignment sheet gives an overview of the project and includes a "choice board" to help students brainstorm ideas for a final product. Creating an Artist Statement asks questions to prompt students' thinking and suggests online resources and examples of artist statements.

Because assigning grades to such varied products can be tricky, I've found it essential to ask students to help me create a scoring guide that will help me fairly assess their work. I use a brainstorming scoring guide to solicit my students' input on their evaluation. I ask students to refer to the original assignment sheet as they complete the brainstorming scoring guide in small groups and report their ideas to rest of the class. Together, we then make a bulleted list of essential components in the areas of content, craft, and conventions. I draft a scoring guide incorporating their suggestions and run it by them for tweaking before creating a final draft.

Keeping Assessment Authentic

The phrase "authentic assessment" gets thrown around often these days and is often code for "anything that isn't an essay." All nontraditional assignments, however, are not created equal. When he created the Darry doll, my sweet teenage son chose the path of least resistance in selecting a nontraditional assignment from the menu of options he'd been provided. But instead of asking students to merely rehash facts or take the least resistant path of completing minimally engaging learning tasks, truly effective assessments must pass this litmus test:

By providing new opportunities to construct knowledge, an assessment ought to *enhance* students' engagement with the text, *enrich* their understanding of themselves and others, and *extend* their hard-earned knowledge into the wider world.

I've seen firsthand evidence that the final projects featured in this chapter meet this litmus test. These projects help students continue learning about the tough texts they've read and reflecting on the civil discourse skills they've practiced. Or to return to the metaphor introduced at the beginning of this chapter, these projects require students to spend the new coin of the realm. Rather than regurgitating memorized facts, students must collaborate with others to solve new problems. They must also synthesize their knowledge and use twenty-first-century skills to communicate what they've learned. And, as an added bonus, no texts are left behind and no Darry dolls need be harmed—or produced—in the process!

Chapter 7

Teachers today must somehow reconcile their own unease and even their own more troubling insights [about society's injustices] with their obligation to initiate their students into a civil society they see as worthy of membership.

—MAXINE GREENE

I once wrote a poem called "Reunion," about a woman who puts one foot in each of two canoes and challenges herself to balance her way down the river. All goes well until the river forks. Rather than choose one course over the other, the woman decides to take both. Her body obediently splits down the center then regenerates itself into two women, each inhabiting her own canoe. The women float in their separate canoes down parallel tributaries that will eventually meet again. In the final stanza of the poem, the narrator wonders,

> *When we get there, my two selves,*
> *will either of us know the other?*
> *Will we reach our weathered hands across*
> *to touch the hollow of full-grown desire*
> *(in the chest and to the left),*
> *to recognize the common rhythm*
> *of the heart?*
> *Will we shake clenched fists,*
> *vow retribution for the thievery?*
> *Or, eyes never meeting, will we rise*
> *from our canoes and walk away*
> *into the forests of our*
> *impenetrable lives, never*
> *to want*
> *to know the difference?*

Advocating for Literacy Learning, Teaching for Social Change

Much like the woman at the start of the poem, I entered the profession with a singular goal—to help my students have richer encounters with texts than many of those I had in school. I wanted my students to do more than answer study questions, read abridged versions of Shakespeare's plays, diagram sentences, write five-paragraph essays, and fill in the correct circles on multiple-choice exams. That is, I wanted to float down the river of my teaching career using progressive pedagogy to challenge what was then the status quo. As a young teacher, I saw few political implications for my teaching beyond expanding the canon to include more diverse voices and media.

The river forked when I entered graduate school. There, I began to realize that every decision I made as a teacher, whether to maintain or challenge the status quo in my classroom, was a political one (Hynds 1997). As always, I insisted that my students come to their own conclusions about what they read and to speak their minds when they wrote, but I split in two as I became more committed to critical literacy. I began thinking seriously about my "obligation to initiate [my] students into a civil society . . . worthy of membership," as Maxine Greene challenges in the epigraph to this chapter. My regenerated self organized literature units deliberately around culturally significant questions, intentionally "teaching the conflicts" as Gerald Graff (1993) would say and encouraging a more critical stance toward the various texts students were reading and creating.

Admittedly, this canoe was less than comfortable at times for both my students and me, but deliberately considering a wider range of perspectives broadened everyone's horizons and sharpened analytical skills. The seemingly simple turn of reshaping a theme like "the American identity" into a question (*What does it mean to be an American?*) made us look at texts in different ways. The question worked as a critical lens through which we could examine varying standpoints, the authors' and our own.

The tributaries still ran parallel to some extent. My students continued to discuss, in small groups, the literature I assigned. I remained at the canoe's stern to steer whole-class discussion of the most controversial texts, largely because I worried that students wouldn't be able to behave themselves when going it alone in rougher rapids.

I still believe that quietly advocating for social change through my teaching methods is important, but studying students' learning experiences and interactions in my classroom eventually taught me that this isn't sufficient if they are ever to climb into their own canoes (see Smagorinsky and O'Donnell-Allen 2000;

Smagorinsky, Daigle, O'Donnell, and Bynum 2010). It wasn't until I conducted teacher research on book clubs in my classroom that I learned that helping students use literature as a vehicle for holding *independent* discussions about provocative issues is in fact our ultimate destination.

If students are ever to exercise critical literacy skills on their own within and beyond my classroom, they need to steer their own craft. That means that I need to advocate for social change more explicitly in my instruction and teach them to advocate for their own literacy learning as well.

Teaching and Learning as Advocacy

The *Oxford English Dictionary* (*OED*) states that in a literal sense, an advocate is one who is "called in, or liable to be called upon, to defend or speak" for someone—a legal client or another person who more generally needs defending—or for something, such as a church or a cause. Another among the many definitions listed for *advocate* in the *OED* that is pertinent here is "one who defends, maintains, publicly recommends, or raises his voice in behalf of a proposal or tenet."

Some in our society may feel that an English teacher's job is to keep both feet planted firmly in one canoe—that is, to teach students to read texts and write correctly and nothing more. But I, like many of you, view teaching as a "calling" to provide students with more than mere instruction in basic literacy skills. Rather, I see it my purpose to advocate, to "call" or "plead" for my students' literacy development and, simultaneously, for social change.

I believe my job as an English teacher is to help my students use their literacies to make changes that will lead to a more just and peaceful world. Teaching them to engage in tough talk about tough texts is one of the best ways I know how.

Advocacy and Tough Texts

In her 1994 speech in which she accepted the Newbery Award for *The Giver*, Lois Lowry (1994) had the following to say about tough texts:

> The man that I named The Giver passed along to the boy knowledge, history, memories, color, pain, laughter, love, and truth. Every time you place a book in the hands of a child, you do the same thing. It is very risky. But each time a child opens a book, he pushes open the gate that separates him from Elsewhere. It gives him choices. It gives him freedom. Those are magnificent, wonderfully unsafe things.

As Lowry's comments suggest, teaching tough texts is risky, but doing so is an essential component of advocacy: these books support students' literacy development in ways that safer texts cannot.

First of all, these are the books kids *want* to read. They're the books that "non-readers" finish and recommend to their teachers because, as Beth, Cam, and Rebecca's students will tell you, they're about real things that matter in students' lives and in the world. Second, tough texts are complex enough that they demand further contemplation. I dare you to read *Life of Pi* (Martel 2001), for instance, without rereading the ending and immediately rethinking the entire book: was Yann Martel just spinning an entertaining adventure story, or was he up to something else? Although tough texts can be appreciated on the basis of plot alone, their complexity invites reasoning through more abstract ideas that matter beyond the book itself.

Of course we still need to teach students about plot structure and character development, but we must also remain mindful that tough texts push us to do something more. When we lose sight of advocacy, even tough texts can get misused as mere vehicles for teaching required concepts or strategies or for preparing students for standardized tests. I sometimes hear teachers say things like, "Oh, I use 'The Most Dangerous Game' to teach them how to label Freytag's pyramid," or, "Poe is good for character analysis." While I can see the logic behind both statements, having taught these texts myself, I can't help wondering what happens to the story in the process. Is there any space left for a deeper exploration of the devastating consequences of an unchecked lust for power in "The Most Dangerous Game" or the corrosive effect of revenge in Poe's "The Cask of Amontillado"?

Tough texts force us to remember that as Robert Coles (1989) argues, "plots offer a psychological or moral journey, with impasses and breakthroughs, with decisions made and destinations achieved." When we focus solely on pedagogically safe concepts like plot and character, we can forget that "a book [can] become for us a signpost, a continuing presence in our lives" (68). Tough texts force us to confront the question one of Coles's students posed, "Why don't all of us—the teachers and the students—try to take these books to *heart*, not just analyze them and then go on to the next book? We may be smarter, but are we better?" (80).

Assigning tough texts and teaching students to read and respond to them qualifies as advocacy because it allows us to address these questions in very real ways. As Lois Lowry reminds us, reading tough texts presents students with choices, with the freedom to make up their own minds about culturally significant issues, not just in literature, but also in their lives. These "wonderfully unsafe things" help them become smarter, more literate individuals who might better the larger world.

Advocacy and Tough Talk

Tough texts invite students to respond in edgy ways, daring them to enter into storied worlds that differ from the reader's own and to use tough talk to explore the perspective of other readers as they do the same. While tough texts prompt students to take a stand, tough talk requires that they learn to listen with openness, speak their minds without fear or malice, and figure out how to deal constructively with the inevitable controversies that arise. Teachers act as advocates for social change when they equip students with tools that help them deal individually, collectively, and civilly with the difficult issues—war, death, identity, religion, race, class, gender—all those elephants in the room that even the grown-ups don't want to face.

Rebecca explained as much to those who, during parent-teacher conferences, questioned her use of tough texts. A few days before one particular conference, Rebecca received an email from a student, Derek, asking to change his book club from *The Curious Incident of the Dog in the Nighttime* (Haddon 2003) to *The Golden Compass* (Pullman 1995) because the profanity used in the former book made him uncomfortable. Aware of the boy's religious background (his father was a minister in a very conservative church), Rebecca reminded Derek that *The Golden Compass* included criticism of organized religion. This was fine with him, he said, because the book had little bad language and he wanted to read it anyway.

Ironically, the switch was fine with Derek's parents as well and for the same reason. At the conference, Rebecca learned that Derek's mother had read all 221 pages of *The Curious Incident* in one night and counted the number of dirty words. She had also heard that one of the other book club choices, *Postcards from No Man's Land*, involved bisexuality. "How do you choose these books?" she wanted to know. "Are you trying to teach your students morals?"

Rebecca explained that she has a combination of reasons for selecting the books students read in civil discourse book clubs: the books have won awards and are school-approved; they qualify as world literature, which is hard to come by in a district curriculum dominated by American titles; and they include adolescent narrators dealing with controversial issues. She also said that while she doesn't "teach morals," students talk about them almost daily in her classroom because the moral choices characters face are central to literature. She mentioned that while direct discussions of morals tend to happen more frequently in connection with contemporary literature since the language is more accessible, morals are front and center in classic literature as well. *Antigone*, for instance, which the class would read later in the year, deals with serious moral issues that have informed concepts central to modern psychoanalytic theory (the Oedipal complex, for example).

Rebecca emphasized that she is careful not to impose her own morals on students. Ultimately, her goal is not to tell students *what* to think, but to provide them with opportunities, like civil discourse book clubs, that *make* them think and allow them to hear viewpoints that may differ from their own. She intentionally chooses books with thorny moral issues because she wants to help kids sort through and learn to articulate where they stand and then communicate their ideas to others respectfully, even when they disagree.

Perhaps because they had engaged in a little civil discourse of their own during this conference, Rebecca and Derek's parents came away from the conference with a better understanding of one another's perspectives. Rebecca understood the parents' concerns, and they were reassured that their son would not be pressured to compromise his religious beliefs. Our field notes and Derek's written responses show that in the end he did not change his views—and that wasn't the point—but he did read *The Golden Compass* carefully; he did engage in heated but respectful book club discussions with his group (one of whom was an agnostic); and he did gain appreciation for other book club members' views.

Systems theorist Margaret Wheatley says, "One of the things we need to learn is that very great change starts from very small conversations, held among people who care." The above example illustrates how all of us advocate for social change when we help our students learn to engage in civil discourse about culturally significant topics, a skill essential to a working democracy.

Advocacy and a Better World

Remember Dragon Boy? He taught Rebecca and me that assigning tough texts is not enough. We must teach students how to talk about them, help them understand the cultural significance of what they are doing, and provide perpetual scaffolding to support them throughout the process. To paraphrase Paolo Freire (1970), all the tools you've read about in this book—starter texts, freewrites, quickreads, sticky-notes, bookmarks, dailies, drop-in conferences, metatalk, and meaningful final projects—help students become not only more competent readers of the *word* but also more critical readers of the *world*.

Freire also said that "one of the most significant abilities we men and women have developed throughout our long history . . . is the possibility of reinventing the world and not simply repeating or reproducing it" (2004, 107). Yet sometimes the world is so much with me that I get overwhelmed. All the social erosion we've seen in recent years—the blatant bigotry, polarized politics, and random violence in schools and communities—seems rooted in an unwillingness to consider other perspectives, listen well and speak peaceably, acknowledge complexity, and respectfully negotiate among varying viewpoints. What can I, one single person, possibly do to change it?

A photograph that hung on the wall of my high school classroom in Oklahoma showed a small boy crouching down near a puddle and cupping a duckling in his hands. The caption read, "To be faithful in small things is a great thing." That's how I've begun thinking about teaching students how to carry on tough talk about tough texts—as a seemingly "small thing" English teachers like you and me can do to have an impact on students' literacy development, their lives, and the world. If students can, with the help of literature, learn to engage in civil discourse, if they can experience working through difficulty rather than collapsing into repression or aggression when it arises, and if they can become advocates for their own learning and the world they want to live in in the process, isn't that also a great thing?

In closing, let me return to "Reunion," to the women in the two canoes. When I think back over my twenty-five years in the classroom, I see two women—the progressive pedagogue and the teacher advocate. To a large extent, progressive pedagogy—writing process methods, reader response strategies, and student-centered teaching—has taken hold in literacy classrooms. And although the pressures of standardized testing have threatened it in recent years, I now see it as part—albeit a very important part—of the status quo. I was an advocate for progressive pedagogy from the very start of my career, but when the river forked at graduate school, I became an advocate for social change through literacy learning. Both teaching selves have made it down the river. Now that we've gotten there, "my two selves, [do] either of us know the other?"

I think they do. Both hold an untarnished passion for teaching and even share many of the same pedagogical values and methods. But the biggest difference is that the teacher advocate has honed, investigated, and amended these methods in service of a much larger cause. The teacher advocate has lost nothing and gained so much more.

In the end, we all get to decide what kind of advocates we will be—advocates for the status quo or advocates for social change. I believe nothing matters more to us as English teachers than helping our students become critical readers and human beings who are willing to understand themselves and one another. It's our way of being advocates, of teaching like our collective future depends on it. It's our way of teaching English to change the world.

Appendix A-1—Is This Book a Tough Text?

Criteria	Questions to Consider
Essential Issues	▪ Does this book focus on significant issues that my students are likely to see as relevant? ▪ Are these issues treated in complex ways? In other words, does the book raise questions about these issues that prompt contemplation rather than encourage easy answers?
Cultural Contexts	▪ Knowing that students ultimately set their own purposes for reading, does this book—and/or students' discussion of it—have potential to challenge or expand students' existing worldviews? ▪ Might it help them look at different cultural contexts from a variety of perspectives and in empathic ways?
Characters	▪ Is the narrator or protagonist, preferably an adolescent, someone with whom my students will connect, even if she or he may differ from them in significant ways (e.g., race, class, gender, background)? ▪ Will my students care about these characters? ▪ Are characters well-developed rather than stereotypical?
Choices, Challenges, and Resolutions	▪ Do the characters wrestle with difficult social, emotional, and moral choices? ▪ Do these choices demand that the characters exercise values and, often, question those values? ▪ Do the challenges presented in the book show the great strength and resilience humans, especially adolescents, are capable of demonstrating? ▪ Does the ending of the book ring true? If the book ends on an ambiguous or down note, does it hold out the possibility of hope or justice, if not for the character then for the reader or the world?
Student Appeal	▪ Is this a book my students would choose to read? ▪ Does this book cry out for conversation? ▪ Will my students see this as a book worth talking about with one another?
Literary Merit	▪ Is this book well crafted? ▪ Does style enhance content through the use of authentic adolescent voices, complex narrative structure, believable dialect, a variety of genres, or other stylistic features? ▪ Has the book earned external recognition, such as awards or outstanding reviews from reputable sources?

Appendix A-2—**Resources for Finding Tough Texts**

Print Resources

Journals with regular reviews of books for adolescents: *ALAN Review*, *English Journal*, *Journal of Adolescent and Adult Literacy*, and *Voices in the Middle*.

Hit List for Young Adults 2: Frequently Challenged Books, by Teri Lesesne and Rosemary Chance for the Young Adult Library Services Association (2002). This follow-up to the 1996 edition of the first *Hit List* features synopses and other resources for twenty YA texts, including lists of articles, awards, reviews, and Internet resources. Also provides various statements on intellectual freedom and readers' rights, information on writing rationales, and tips for dealing with censorship.

Making the Match, by Teri Lesesne (2003). Provides a number of booklists, arranged by genre, subject, and theme, such as Multicultural Books, Books for 21st-Century Teens, Books to Accompany Havighurst's Developmental Tasks, YA Literature from Laughter to Tears, and Tough Books for Tough Times.

Radical Reads: 101 Young Adult Novels on the Edge, by Joni Bodart (2002). Includes lists of YA books published between 1990–2001 on controversial topics that adolescents are likely to find relevant. Annotated entries include plot summaries, controversial topics, character descriptions, excerpts of reviews, awards, reading levels, and soforth. Also provides tips for booktalks and writing curricular rationales. (Bodart's Booktalk series also includes brief summaries of books for students.)

Teenplots, by John Gillespie and Corinne Naden (2003). Annotations of 100 books appropriate for adolescents. Arranged by genres and themes, entries include plot summaries, main characters, themes and subjects, author information, and lists of other suggested texts.

Theme-Sets for Secondary Students: How to Scaffold Core Literature, by Jeanine Richison, Anita Hernandez, and Marcia Carter (2006). Provides lists of thematically related poems, short stories, plays, and other genres to accompany canonical novels. Themes include migrant families, growing up ethnic in America, literature of war, the bullying mentality, and utopian/dystopian societies.

Web Resources
Award-Winning Books for Young Adults

These websites post the following awards:

American Library Association (ALA)

- Coretta Scott King Award. Awarded annually since 1970 to African American authors and illustrators of books for young readers (www.ala.org/ala/mgrps/rts/emiert/cskbookawards/index.cfm)
- John Steptoe New Talent Award. Awarded annually since 2009 to African American authors and illustrators of books for young readers who have published three or fewer published works (same URL as above).
- Newbery Medal. Awarded annually since 1922 for the most distinguished children's book published in the previous year (www.ala.org/ala/mgrps/divs/alsc/awardsgrants/bookmedia/newberymedal/newberyhonors/newberymedal.cfm).

The Cybils: The Children's and Young Adult Bloggers' Literary Awards Awarded annually by bloggers who write about children's and YA literature that combine high literary merit with "kid appeal" (http://dadtalk.typepad.com/cybils/).

Young Adult Library Services Association website (YALSA) www.ala.org/ala/mgrps/divs/yalsa/booklistsawards/booklistsbook.cfm

- Alex Award. Awarded annually since 1998 to ten books that although written for adults are likely to appeal to adolescents.
- Margaret A. Edwards Award. Awarded annually since 1998 to honor the lifetime contributions of a YA author and a specific body of her or his work.
- Michael L. Printz Award. Awarded annually since 2000 to a YA book of literary merit.
- William C. Morris YA Debut Award. Awarded annually since 2009 to a debut YA book published by a first-time author.

Award-Winning Authors for Young Adults

The website for the Assembly on Literature for Adolescents (ALAN) (www.alan-ya.org/) posts the following awards:

- ALAN Award. Awarded annually to authors who have made outstanding contributions to the field of YA literature.
- Amelia Elizabeth Walden Award. Awarded annually to the author of a fictional book, preferably a novel, considered to be the year's most relevant title for young adults.

Book Lists

These websites post the following lists of recommended books for YA readers:

Young Adult Library Services Association website (YALSA) www.ala.org/ala/mgrps/divs/yalsa/ booklistsawards/booklistsbook.cfm

- Alex Awards
- Amazing Audiobooks for Young Adults
- Best Books for Young Adults
- Best Fiction for Young Adults
- Best of the Best Books for Young Adults
- Great Graphic Novels for Teens
- Popular Paperbacks for Young Adults
- Outstanding Books for the College Bound
- Quick Picks for Reluctant Readers
- Teens' Top Ten

American Library Services to Children (ALSC)

www.ala.org/ala/mgrps/divs/alsc/index.cfm
- Notable Books (for children through age 14)

Children's Book Council (CBC)   www.cbcbooks.org/

- Hot off the Press (a monthly list of anticipated bestsellers)
- Showcase (a thematic list of books posted quarterly)
- Children's Choices (chosen yearly by five teams of children through sixth grade)

guysread.com

- Jon Scieszka's site "to help boys find stuff they like to read."

International Reading Association

www.reading.org/Resources/Booklists.aspx
- Young Adults' Choices
- Teachers' Choices

readingrants.org

- Features "out of the ordinary booklists for teens," such as Nail Biters, Riot Grrrl!, Slacker Fiction, and Inquiring Minds Want To Know; also includes yearly Top Ten lists, reviews written by teens, and links to teen-lit blogs and websites.

teenreads.com

- Cool New Books
- Ultimate Reading List

Appendix A-3—**Anticipating Challenges to Tough Texts: Some Resources That Can Help**

Books

Brown, J. 1994. *Preserving Intellectual Freedom: Fighting Censorship in Our Schools.* Urbana, IL: NCTE.

Pipkin, G., and R. C. Lent. 2002. *At the Schoolhouse Gate: Lessons in Intellectual Freedom.* Portsmouth, NH: Heinemann.

Power, B. M., J. D. Wilhelm, and K. Chandler. 1997. *Reading Stephen King: Issues of Censorship, Student Choice, and Popular Literature.* Urbana, IL: NCTE.

Rationales for Challenged Books. Volumes 1 and 2. Prepared by NCTE in Partnership with IRA. Compact Disc.

Reid., L., and J. Neufeld. 1999. *Rationales for Teaching Young Adult Literature.* Portsmouth, NH: Heinemann.

Journals

English Journal (See issues published February 1997, November 1999, January 2001, January 2008.)

Journal of Adolescent and Adult Literacy (See issues published December 2000/January 2001, February 2002, March 2006, May 2009.)

Websites

American Library Association (ALA)—Banned and Challenged Books
www.ala.org/ala/issuesadvocacy/banned/index.cfm

- Yearly lists of Top Ten Most Challenged Books
- Banned Book Week information and materials
- Resources for dealing with challenges to library materials, many of which are also applicable to the classroom

ALA—Intellectual Freedom for Young People

www.ala.org/ala/aboutala/offices/oif/foryoungpeople/youngpeople.cfm
Information and links to numerous websites exploring the First Amendment rights of young people in schools.

ALA Office for Intellectual Freedom

www.ala.org/ala/aboutala/offices/oif/index.cfm
Statements, policies, and toolkits on intellectual freedom, quotations on the First Amendment and the freedom to read, and information on censorship in schools.

As If! (Authors Support Intellectual Freedom)

http://asifnews.blogspot.com/
Blog by several YA authors championing those who stand against censorship of YA books.

Judy Blume Talks About Censorship

http://judyblume.com/censorship.php
Thoughts on and tips for dealing with censorship for students, teachers, libraries, and authors.

International Reading Association Resolution on the Selection of Reading Materials

www.reading.org/Libraries/Resources/On_Selection_Of_Rdg_Materials_1.pdf
Statement and policy recommendations on selecting texts and responding to challenges.

Kidspeak!

www.kidspeakonline.org/index.htm
Created in response to outrage over banning Harry Potter books. Includes up-to-date news on censorship cases, kids' responses to censorship issues, a censorship IQ test, and tips for dealing with censorship.

Appendix A-3 cont.

National Coalition against Censorship

www.ncac.org/

General information, news, and resources for dealing with censorship, including a "Book Censorship in Schools Resource Guide/Toolkit" and resource guides on the First Amendment rights of schools, teachers, and parents.

National Council of Teachers of English (NCTE) Anti-Censorship Center

www.ncte.org/action/anti-censorship

Advice, documents, and other resources for teachers dealing with challenges to literary works, films and videos, drama productions, or teaching methods.

Random House Website

- *First Amendment First-Aid Kit*

  www.randomhouse.com/teens/firstamendment/index.html

  Lists of banned books, strategies for dealing with book challenges, YA authors' thoughts on censorship, tips for discussions on censorship, other resources including sample letter to the editor, links to organizations that can provide support in the case of book challenges, and PDF files of First Amendment and "Censorship Causes Blindness" poster.

- *Teacher's Guide on Censorship*

  www.randomhouse.com/highschool/resources/guides3/censorship.html

  Teaching ideas, essay topics, and lists of censored books.

Appendix A-4—Checkpoint Scoring Guide

I use a checkpoint system to evaluate your responses so that I can return them to you quickly and so that you'll know how you're doing. Occasionally, I'll just give you credit (a "check") for completing the assignment, but usually you'll find one of the following symbols at the top of the page. Here's what they mean:

✔ <u>Check</u>: You earn a check when you complete the minimum requirements for the assignment in a *thoughtful and thorough* manner. Even though you're exploring your ideas on paper, your writing is clear enough that I can easily understand your ideas. You get full credit for a check.

✔+ <u>Check-Plus</u>: You earn a check-plus when you go above and beyond the minimum requirements in some way. You might write an idea that helps me understand something about the text that I didn't already know before. You might ask a great question and think about some possible answers, or you may have explained your ideas really well. In other words, you've taken risks in your thinking and great care in your writing and it shows. You get extra credit for a check-plus.

✔– <u>Check-Minus</u>: You earn a check-minus when one or more of the following problems exists: You haven't met the minimum requirements of the assignment. Your response feels neither *thoughtful* nor *thorough*. Instead, it feels like you're simply going through the motions to get your homework done. Your writing is so unclear that I can't understand the gist of what you're saying. I deduct points for a check-minus.

Appendix A-5—**Field Notes Journal**

DATE _____

CLASS _____

OBSERVATIONS	REFLECTIONS
What's happening here?	What do I think about it? What questions does it raise?

TO THINK ABOUT

What are my overall impressions of how the groups went today? What do I need to think about further? Are any needs, patterns, or questions consistently emerging? Do I need to take any specific action before students meet again?

May be copied for classroom use. © 2011 by Cindy O'Donnell-Allen from *Tough Talk, Tough Texts* (Portsmouth, NH: Heinemann).

Appendix B-1—**How to Construct Your Bookmark**

1. Use your scissors to cut along the outer edges of your bookmark.

2. Fold the whole bookmark in half *vertically* so that the printed part is on the *inside*. In other words, the open edges will be on the *right*, and you *won't* be able to see the print. When you open your bookmark back up, it will now have an invisible fold line down the middle.

3. Once you've opened your bookmark back up, make folds on the *printed* vertical lines that form the columns. This time, fold the printed parts to the *outside* so that one column is overlapping the other. At this point, your bookmark should be the shape of a candy bar or a brochure.

4. Now open the bookmark back up, and fold it down the middle "invisible" vertical line again. But this time, fold it the opposite way from the way you did before so that the printed part is on the *outside*. In other words, the open edges will be on the left, and you can still see all the print.

5. Tape the outer open edges together only on the left side. *Do not tape the top and bottom edges!* These will remain open for a reason.

6. Now press the inside printed folds of the bookmark back into the middle so that it looks sort of like a hot dog bun.

7. You're finished! On one side of the "bun," you should be able to see your reading schedule. On the other side of the "bun," you can see the sticky-note prompts But if you open up the bookmark to look inside the "bun," you can still read the "what's up with the sticky notes" part in the middle where the "hot dog" would be.

Appendix B-2—**Dailies Form for High School Students**

Sticky Notes	Responses to My Sticky Notes (Not sure what to say? Take a look at the prompts on your sticky-notes bookmark.)
Put your sticky notes here! (If you need to, stack them.)	

METATALK

1. Talk about your talk. What controversial subjects did you talk about in book club today? List them below.

_____   _____   _____

2. Circle the most important topic. Why is it most important?

Appendix B-2 cont.

METATALK—Side Two	
How _I_ responded to the _controversial topic_ **in our discussion** (describe specific reactions)	**How _my group_ responded to the** _controversial topic_ **in our discussion** (describe specific reactions)
What _I_ need to keep doing or should do next time so we can have an effective discussion of controversial topics	**What _my group_ needs to keep doing or should do next time so we can have an effective discussion of controversial topics**

May be copied for classroom use. © 2011 by Cindy O'Donnell-Allen from _Tough Talk, Tough Texts_ (Portsmouth, NH: Heinemann).

Appendix B-2   Dailies Form for High School Students

Appendix B-3—**Dailies Form for Middle School Students**

Sticky Notes	Responses to My Sticky Notes
	This part of the book made me . . . (circle one or more of the words below OR fill in the blank)
Put your sticky notes here. **(You can stack them** **if you need to.)**	think blink wonder feel understood laugh cry confused nervous _____ *And here's why . . .*

METATALK:

1. Talk about your talk. What controversial subjects did you talk about in book club today? List them below.

_____   _____   _____

2. Circle the most important topic. Why is it most important?

TURN THE PAGE OVER

Appendix B-3 cont.

METATALK (Continued)	
HOW MY GROUP DID (describe how YOUR GROUP responded to the controversial topic in book club)	**HOW I DID** (describe how YOU responded to the topic during book club)
WHAT MY GROUP NEEDS **TO DO NEXT TIME** (describe what YOUR GROUP could do to make your discussion more effective)	**WHAT I NEED TO DO** **NEXT TIME** (describe what YOU could do to make your discussion more effective)

May be copied for classroom use. © 2011 by Cindy O'Donnell-Allen from *Tough Talk, Tough Texts* (Portsmouth, NH: Heinemann).

References

Aikin, J. 1796. Aphorisms on mind and manners. *The Monthly Magazine, or British Register, 3,* 178–79.

Allington, R. L. 2007. Effective teachers, effective instruction. In *Adolescent literacy: Turning promise into practice,* eds. K. Beers, R. E. Probst, and L. Rief, 273–88. Portsmouth, NH: Heinemann.

Anderson, J. 2005. *Mechanically inclined: Building grammar, usage, and style into writer's workshop.* Portsmouth, NH: Heinemann.

Anderson, M. T. 2004. *Feed.* Cambridge, MA: Candlewick Press.

Anstéy, M., and G. Bull. 2006. *Teaching and learning multiliteracies: Changing times, changing literacies.* Newark, DE: International Reading Association.

Atwell, N. 2007. *The reading zone: How to help kids become skilled, passionate, habitual, critical readers.* New York: Scholastic.

Austin, J. L. 1962. *How to do things with words.* Oxford, England: Clarendon Press.

Barnes, D. 1992. *From communication to curriculum.* 2nd ed. Portsmouth, NH: Heinemann.

Beers, K. 2002. *When kids can't read, what teachers can do.* Portsmouth, NH: Heinemann.

Bishop, S. 2003. A sense of place. In *Rural voices: Place-conscious education and the teaching of writing,* ed. Brooke, R., 65–82. New York: Teachers College Press.

Bomer, R. 2007. The role of handover in teaching for democratic participation. In *Adolescent literacy: Turning promise into practice,* eds. K. Beers, R. E. Probst, and L. Rief, 303–10. Portsmouth, NH: Heinemann.

Bruner, J. 1975. From communication to language: A psychological perspective. *Cognition, 3,* 255–87.

———. 1996. *The culture of education.* Cambridge, MA: Harvard University Press.

Burke, K. 1968. Psychology and form. In *Counter-Statement.* 2nd ed. Berkeley: University of California Press.

Carlsen, G. R. 1967/1980. *Books and the teenage reader.* New York: Harper.

Carroll, P. S. 1997. Today's teens, their problems, and their literature: Revisiting G. Robert Carlsen's *Books and the teenage reader* thirty years later. *English Journal, 86*(3), 25–34.

Carter, B. 2000. *Best books for young adults.* 2nd ed. Chicago: American Library Association.

Carter, M., N. Mota-Altman, and F. Peitzman. 2009. *Creating spaces for study and action under the social justice umbrella.* Berkeley, CA: National Writing Project.

Chambers, A. 1999. *Postcards from no man's land.* New York: Speak.

Chbosky, S. 1999. *The perks of being a wallflower.* New York: Simon and Schuster.

Christensen, L. 2000. *Reading, writing, and rising up: Teaching about social justice and the power of the written word.* Milwaukee, WI: Rethinking Schools.

Cochran-Smith, M., and S. Lytle. 2009. *Inquiry as stance: Practitioner research in the next generation.* New York: Teachers College Press.

Coles, R. 1989. *The call of stories: Teaching and the moral imagination.* Boston: Houghton Mifflin.

Cone, J. 2003. Constructing urban high school students as achievers. Retrieved from http://gallery.carnegiefoundation.org/collections/castl_k12/jcone/index2.html.

Cormier, R. 1974. *The chocolate war.* New York: Random House.

Daniels, H. 2002. *Literature circles: Voice and choice in book clubs and reading groups.* Portland, ME: Stenhouse.

Diamond, B. J., and M. A. Moore. 1995. *Multicultural literacy: Mirroring the reality of the classroom.* New York: Longman.

Douglass, F. *Narrative of the life of Frederick Douglass: An American slave, written by himself.* New York: Bedford/St. Martin's.

Early, M. 1960. Stages of growth in literary appreciation. *English Journal, 49*(3), 161–67.

Esman, A. H. 1990. *Adolescence and culture.* New York: Columbia University Press.

Finders, M. 1997. *Just girls: Hidden literacies and life in junior high.* New York: Teachers College Press.

Freire, P. 1970. *Pedagogy of the oppressed.* New York: Seabury.

———. 1998. *Pedagogy of freedom: Ethics, democracy, and civic courage.* New York: Rowman and Littlefield.

———. 2004. *Pedagogy of indignation.* Boulder, CO: Paradigm.

Fu, D. 2009. *Writing between languages: How English language learners make the transition to fluency, grades 4–12.* Portsmouth, NH: Heinemann.

Gallagher, K. 2009. *Readicide: How schools are killing reading and what you can do about it.* Portland, ME: Stenhouse.

Gallas, K. 1997. *"Sometimes I can be anything": Power, gender, and identity in a primary classroom.* New York: Teachers College Press.

Gardner, H. 1996. *Leading minds: An anatomy of leadership.* New York: Basic Books.

Gay, G. 2000. *Culturally responsive teaching: Theory, research, and practice.* New York: Teachers College Press.

Graff, G. 1993. *Beyond the culture wars: How teaching the conflicts can revitalize American education.* New York: W.W. Norton.

Green, J. 2005. *Looking for Alaska.* New York: Speak.

Greene, M. 1977. Toward wide-awakeness: An argument for the arts and humanities in education. *Teachers College Record, 79*(1), 119–25.

———. 1995. Art and imagination: Overcoming a desperate stasis. *Phi Delta Kappan, 76*(1), 378–82.

———. 2007. Countering indifference: The role of the arts. Retrieved from www.maxinegreene.org/articles.php.

Habegger, L. 2004. Why are realistic young adult novels so bleak?: An analysis of bleak realism in *A step from heaven*. *Indiana Libraries, 23*(2), 34–40.

Haddon, C. 2003. *The curious incident of the dog in the nighttime.* New York: Vintage.

Hartman, P. 2006. "Loud on the inside": Working-class girls, gender, and literacy. *Research in the Teaching of English, 41,* 82–117.

Haskell, R. E. 2000. *Transfer of learning: Cognition, instruction, and reasoning.* San Diego, CA: Academic Press.

Heaven, P. 1994. *Contemporary adolescence: A social psychological approach.* South Melbourne, Australia: Macmillan.

Herrington, A., K. Hodgson, and C. Moran, Eds. 2009. *Teaching the new writing: Technology, change, and assessment in the 21st-century classroom.* New York: Teachers College Press.

Hicks, T. 2009. *The digital writing workshop.* Portsmouth, NH: Heinemann.

Hinton, S. E. 1967. *The Outsiders.* New York: Puffin.

Holtgraves, T. 2002. *Language as social action: Social psychology and language use.* Mahwah, NJ: Erlbaum.

Hynds, S. 1997. *On the brink: Negotiating literature and life with adolescents.* New York: Teachers College Press.

Johnson, A. 2010. *Heaven.* New York: Simon and Schuster.

Kajder, S. 2007. Unleashing potential with emerging technologies. In *Adolescent literacy: Turning promise into practice*, eds. K. Beers, R. E. Probst, and L. Rief, 213–30. Portsmouth, NH: Heinemann.

Kauer, S. M. 2008. A battle reconsidered: Second thoughts on book censorship and conservative parents. *English Journal, 97*(3), 56–60.

Kay, K. 2008. Learning to change, changing to learn. Retrieved from www.pearson foundation.org/pg5.6.html.

Keene, E. O. 2008. *To understand: New horizons in reading comprehension.* Portsmouth, NH: Heinemann.

Kirkland, D. 2009. Researching and teaching English in the digital dimension. *Research in the Teaching of English, 44,* 8–22.

Leander, K. 2006. Wired bodies in wireless classrooms. In *A new literacies sampler*, eds. M. Knobel and C. Lankshear, 25–48. New York: Peter Lang.

Lent, R. C. 2008. Facing the issues: Challenges, censorship, and reflection through dialogue. *English Journal, 97*(3), 61–66.

Lesesne, T. S. 2003. *Making the match: The right book for the right reader at the right time, grades 4–12.* Portland, MN: Stenhouse.

———. 2007. Of times, teens, and books. In *Adolescent literacy: Turning promise into practice*, eds. K. Beers, R. E. Probst, and L. Rief, 61–79. Portsmouth, NH: Heinemann.

Lesesne, T. S., and R. Chance. 2002. *Hit list for young adults 2: Frequently challenged books.* Chicago: Young Adult Library Services Association.

Lowry, L. 1993. *The giver.* New York: Delacorte Press.

———. 1994. Excerpt from 1994 Newbery acceptance speech for *The giver.* Retrieved from www.loislowry.com/pdf/Newbery_Award.pdf.

———. 2000. *Gathering blue.* New York: Delacorte Press.

Marshall, J. D., P. Smagorinsky, and M. W. Smith. 1994. *The language of interpretation: Patterns of discourse in discussions of literature.* Urbana, IL: National Council of Teachers of English.

Martel, Y. 2001. *Life of Pi.* Boston, MA: HarcourtBooks.

Meyer, S. 2008. *Twilight.* New York: Little, Brown Books for Young Readers.

National Council of the Teachers of English. 1981. Guideline on the students' right to read. Retrieved from www.ncte.org/positions/statements/righttoread guideline.

National Council of the Teachers of English Anti-Censorship Center. (n.d.) How to write a rationale. Retrieved from www.ncte.org/action/anti-censorship /rationales.

National Council of Teachers of English and the International Reading Association. 1996. *Standards for the English language arts.* Newark, DE: International Reading Association.

Oakes, J. 2005. *Keeping track: How schools structure inequality.* New Haven, CT: Yale University Press.

Oatley, K. 2005. A feeling for fiction. *Greater Good, 2*(2), 13–15.

O'Donnell-Allen, C. 2005. Pedagogical recycling: How colleagues change colleagues' minds. *English Journal, 95*(2), 58–64.

———. 2006. *The book club companion: Fostering strategic readers in the secondary classroom.* Portsmouth, NH: Heinemann.

Oldfather, P. 1993. *Students' perspectives on motivating experiences in literacy learning.* Perspectives in Reading Research No. 2. Athens, GA: Universities of Georgia and Maryland, National Reading Research Center.

Palmer, P. 2004. *A hidden wholeness: The journey toward an undivided life.* San Francisco: Jossey-Bass.

Paterson. K. 1977/1987. *Bridge to Terabithia.* New York: HarperTrophy.

Paton, A. 1948. *Cry, the beloved country.* New York: Scribner.

Pew Internet and American Life Project. 2008. *Writing, technology, and teens.* Retrieved from www.writingcommission.org.

Plath, Sylvia. 1963. *The Bell Jar.* London: Heinemann.

Porter, C. R. 2000. *Imani all mine.* New York: Mariner Books.

Pritchett. L. 2005. *Sky bridge.* Minneapolis, MN: Milkweed Editions.

Probst, R. E. 2007. Tom Sawyer, Teaching and Talking. In *Adolescent literacy: Turning promise into practice*, eds. K. Beers, R. E. Probst, and L. Rief, 43–59. Portsmouth, NH: Heinemann.

Public Broadcasting System. 1999. Treasures of the world. Retrieved from www.pbs.org/treasuresoftheworld/guernica/gmain.html.

Pullman, P. 1995. *The golden compass.* New York: Random House.

Reeves, A. R. 2004. *Adolescents talk about reading: Exploring resistance to and engagement with text.* Newark, NJ: International Reading Association.

Rose, M. 2005. *Lives on the boundary.* New York: Penguin.

————. 2009. *Why school? Reclaiming education for all of us*. New York: The New Press.

Rosenblatt, L. 1978/1994. *The reader, the text, the poem*. Carbondale: Southern Illinois University Press.

Searle, J. R. 1969. *Speech acts*. Cambridge, UK: Cambridge University Press.

Sipe, R., and T. Rosewarne. 2006. *Purposeful writing: Genre study in the secondary writing workshop*. Portsmouth, NH: Heinemann.

Smagorinsky, P., E. A. Daigle, C. O'Donnell-Allen, and S. Bynum. 2010. Bullshit in academic writing: A Protocol analysis of a high school senior's process of interpreting *Much Ado about Nothing*. *Research in the Teaching of English, 44*, 368–405.

Smagorinsky, P., and C. O'Donnell-Allen. 1998. Reading as mediated and mediating action: Composing meaning for literature through multimedia interpretive texts. *Reading Research Quarterly, 33*(2), 198–226.

————. 2000. Idiocultural diversity in small groups: The role of the relational framework in collaborative learning. In *Vygotskian perspectives on literacy research: Constructing meaning through collaborative inquiry*, eds. C. D. Lee and P. Smagorinsky, 165–90. New York: Cambridge University Press.

Smith, M. W., and J. Wilhelm, J. 2006. *Going with the flow: How to engage boys (and girls) in their literacy learning*. Portsmouth, NH: Heinemann.

Spinelli, J. 2003. *Loser*. New York: HarperCollins.

————. 2004. *Wringer*. New York: HarperTeen.

Stafford, W. 1986. *You must revise your life*. Ann Arbor: University of Michigan.

Steiner, G. 1978. *On difficulty and other essays*. New York: Oxford University Press.

Tatum, A. W. 2006. Engaging African American males in reading. *Educational Leadership, 63*(5), 44–49.

Tsujimoto, J. 1988. *Teaching poetry writing to adolescents*. Urbana, IL: NCTE.

Vygotsky, L. S. 1978. *Mind in society: The development of higher psychological processes*. Boston: Harvard University Press.

Walker, A. 1982. *The color purple.* New York: Harcourt Brace Jovanovich.

Wheatley, M. 2000. Turning to one another. Keynote address for Kansas Health Foundation 2000 Leadership Institute. Retrieved from www.margaretwheatley .com/articles/turningtooneanother.html.

Wiggins, G., and J. McTighe. 2005. *Understanding by design,* 2nd ed. Upper Saddle River, NJ: Pearson.

Wittgenstein, L. 1953. *Philosophical investigations.* Oxford, England: Blackwell.

Wood, D., J. Bruner, and G. Ross. 1976. The role of tutoring in problem solving. *Journal of child psychology and psychiatry, 17,* 89–100.

Questions for Group Study

First, a confession: from my second year of teaching on, I've taken a hard-line stance against book study questions for my students. That's because during my first year, I discovered that in digging through the text to write them, I was the one doing all the hard interpretive work. The questions weren't much more than a thinly veiled classroom management tool that I as a new teacher needed to help students stay on task in small groups. From my second year on, however, I told my students to come with something to say about the text they were reading and taught them response strategies to guarantee they would do so.

Fast-forward a couple of decades later to my own book club experience with other adults. Even though everyone came to our meetings with something to say, more often than not, it wasn't about the book. Our passing attempts amounted to little more than, "Did you like the book?" before we moved on to more "important" matters like, "How's your back?" At one meeting my friend Denise was fed up; she turned to the "reader's guide" at the back of the book and started asking questions. And . . . it worked. For the first time in our book club's history, we actually talked about the book for more than five whole minutes. Turns out that we—independent adult readers—needed a classroom management tool of sorts. The guide was a useful starting point that helped us stay on track.

I offer these questions for group study in the same spirit. I don't suggest that you work down the list of questions slavishly but rather that you use them insofar as they help deepen your thinking and/or keep your discussion focused on the book. You may want to preview the questions before you begin a chapter as a way of framing your reading, divide the questions up among you so each person is reading with only one question in mind, or star a few after you've finished reading that you'd really like to take up with your colleagues.

By all means consider your own questions as well or use any methods you would use otherwise as a reader—sticky notes, marginalia, dog-eared pages, and the like. You may also want to try dailies or another response strategy you regularly assign your students. (Nothing like completing your own assignment to determine whether it helps you engage with a text or only amounts to busy work!)

Teachers who've read *The Book Club Companion* have told me that they also like a strategy I feature in that book called the "punctuation prompt." The method is simple: pencil a *question mark* in the margin when you come to an idea that makes you wonder, a *comma* when you find a passage that gives you pause, and an *exclamation point* when you have a strong reaction to something you've read. Then when discussion rolls around, simply flip back through the chapter and choose one or two items that seem most critical for your group to discuss.

Whatever response method you choose, what's most important is that you come to the discussion with something to say and with an openness to what others think, too.

Oh, one more thing: to maintain that openness in your group and to honor everyone's precious time, I strongly recommend setting some group norms for interaction and accountability prior to your first discussion. Would that it were not so, but adults need them at least as much as kids do. The questions in Figure 5.1, Goals and Ground Rules, can help get you started.

Introduction

1. A six-word memoir challenges writers to tell their life stories in a mere six words.[1] Try out the genre by using six words to explain why you became an English teacher, then share your six-word memoir with others in your study group. What has remained constant about your original motivation and what has changed? Do you believe English teachers can change the world? How does your opinion shape your work with students?

---

[1]The six-word memoir is said to have originated with Ernest Hemingway's perhaps briefest story: *For sale: Baby shoes, never worn*. Taking their cue from Hemingway, Larry Smith and the creators of the online *Smith Magazine* created the Six-Word Memoirs Project, publishing best-selling anthologies and websites of six-word memoirs on various themes. Read more at www.smithmag.net/sixwords/.

2. Think about a controversial issue or cultural conflict that has arisen in your classroom or school recently. How did your students deal with it? What have you observed about how your students deal with these issues outside school? What role models do your students have for dealing with controversy? Would you describe these role models as positive, negative, or somewhere in between? What are the implications for your teaching?

3. As described on page xiv, high school students in Rebecca Garrett's English class contended that teachers should share their views on controversial issues as long as they don't impose those views on students. Do you agree or disagree? If a student asked your opinion in class about a controversial issue, how would you respond? Why?

4. One way of thinking about achieving social justice in education is to increase equity and access for all students so that they can build a more socially just world in turn. What part might students' literacy practices play in working toward this goal? What does this mean for your teaching?

Chapter 1

1. As I point out in this chapter, the oft-used term *civil discourse* is seldom, if ever, defined, suggesting that people "know civil discourse when they see it," or perhaps more often when they don't. What is your definition of *civil discourse*? What does it look like in a classroom setting? What does it look like outside of school? How does your definition of the term compare to the bulleted list on page 12? What would you add or omit from this list?

2. Aphorisms like "talk is cheap" and "actions speak louder than words" suggest that talk and action are separate entities. Do you agree or disagree with this claim? Is it possible for talk to be a form of action in and of itself?

3. When you look at the characteristics of tough texts described on page 14, how do you feel about asking students to read them in your classroom? What are the risks and benefits? How does your teaching context influence what you are able to teach? What challenges do you anticipate in teaching tough texts in your school?

Chapter 2

1. How would you have responded to the questions posed by the workshop participant in the first paragraph of this chapter? What do your responses reveal about the books you assign your students?

2. What literary texts engage your students most? What books do they "take to heart"? What do those texts have in common? What evidence do you have that the books you assign make a difference to students' lives beyond your classroom?

3. Do you assign young adult literature? Why or why not? What observations do you have about the crossover between YA literature and mainstream fiction and how it might benefit your students?

4. At the confirmation hearings for her seat on the Supreme Court, some legislators criticized Justice Sonia Sotomayor's assertion that empathy helped her judge more fairly. Is the capacity for empathy a liability in today's world? What role do you observe empathy playing in students' reading processes, their learning, and their interactions with peers?

Chapter 3

1. Which of the books that you have taught over the years have had the greatest impact on students? What about those books made them worth teaching for you and worth remembering for students?

2. What are some essential cultural issues you believe students might productively address by reading tough texts? What are some books you don't currently teach that could help students view these issues from various perspectives?

3. By definition, tough texts deal with thorny issues and often have ambiguous endings. If you observed students in a small group who were struggling through a rough patch in the book, how much would you intervene?

4. In this chapter, I argue that "there are books you teach to a whole class, those you make available to small groups, and others you recommend to individual students." Considering your teaching context, can you think of one book in each category? Why would you label these books in these ways?

5. What would you do if a parent formally challenged a book you were teaching or recommended that it be banned from the school library or curriculum? Are there books you would be willing to "go to the mat" for, even if you met resistance from students and parents? What makes these books worthwhile?

Chapter 4

1. Take a look Figure 1.1: What Is *Civil Discourse*? Have you seen similar scenarios when students work in small-group discussions? How have they played out? How might you use the strategies in this chapter to help students work through such conflicts?

2. If you agree that quickwrites could be useful for your students through-out a CDS, which, if any, of the strategies from this chapter might you use to deal with the paperload? What are some other grading strategies you've tried that will allow your students to write as much as they need to and still allow you to "have a life" at the same time?

3. Brainstorm as many potential starter texts as you can. With good col-leagues nearby and a pencil in hand, make some preliminary plans for selecting and sequencing the texts in a CDS by working through the questions on page 67.

4. Whether you use sticky notes or not, how do you help students learn to read texts closely on their own?

5. How might you use the think-aloud strategy with your students? What's a text you might use? Knowing that students could get overwhelmed if you modeled every thinking strategy that you use, what processes would you emphasize?

Chapter 5

1. Do you feel more comfortable assigning one tough text to the entire class for a CDS or dividing students into book clubs to discuss a text of their choice? When and why would you use one method over the other?

2. *If you're considering the whole-class option,* which of the recommended strategies would you use to divide students in groups? Why does this method seem more appealing to you than the others, or does the method depend on the class?

3. *If you're considering the book club option,* think about a book you might like to use and, with good colleagues nearby and a pencil in hand, sketch out a booktalk, using the list on pages 86–87 to prompt your thinking.

4. Do you think you'll frontload the norming process like Beth and Rebecca do or weave it throughout the CDS as Cam does? Why does this choice seem most appropriate for your classroom?

5. Depending on the grade level you teach, take a look at the sticky-notes bookmark for middle school students (Figure 5.2) or high school students (Figure 4.3). How would you use or modify the prompts in panel three to help your students tackle the range of difficulties readers encounter (Steiner 1978; see also Figure 4.1)? What are some other prompts you might add?

6. Think back over small-group discussions you've observed in your classroom, and identify an incident when a drop-in visit would be in order. How did you respond? If a similar incident occurred in the future, what amount of endoscaffolding would be most judicious? How will you judge when to intervene and when to let students work out the problem on their own?

Chapter 6

1. Reread the epigraph at the opening of this chapter. Think about the typical kind of assessment you were asked to complete at the end of literature units in your English classes *as a student.* How well does it

align with the twenty-first-century skill set Ken Kay describes as the "new coin of the realm"? Now think about a recent assessment you asked your own students to complete at the end of a literature unit. How well does it align? What are the implications of these comparisons for your teaching and your students' learning?

2. Which of the projects in this chapter can you imagine using in your classroom at the end of a CDS? Would you use them as is, or would you adapt the assignments? If so, what would these be?

3. One of the primary goals of all of the response strategies and assignments in this book is to help students transfer the civil discourse skills they have developed in the course of a CDS to settings outside school. To meet this goal, students must be aware of the skills they are using. How can you build a reflective component into the final assessments you ask students to complete at the end of a CDS?

4. All of the projects in this chapter are multimodal to some degree. That is, they require students to use print, visual images, digital tools, and/or verbal means to demonstrate their knowledge. How will you deal with concerns that colleagues, parents, or even students might raise that nontraditional forms of assessment like these are not academically rigorous?

5. How do you define "authentic assessment"? Who determines whether an assessment is "authentic"? What does authentic assessment look like in your teaching?

Chapter 7

1. Was there a time when the river forked in your teaching and you had to decide what kind of teacher you wanted to be? What happened? How have the decisions you have made in the moment affected the teacher you are today?

2. How central should advocacy, as it is defined in this chapter, be to teachers' work with students? Why do you think so? Do you consider yourself a teacher advocate? If not, why not? If so, what do you advocate for?

3. In my study at home where I wrote much of this book, I have a sticky note affixed over my desk that reads, "Is it possible to be gently radical?" How would you respond to this question in relation to your teaching? What relationship do you see between academic rigor and social change?

4. Why does it matter whether students learn to engage in civil discourse in and beyond your classroom?

5. Paolo Freire said, "One of the most significant abilities we men and women have developed throughout our long history . . . is the possibility of reinventing the world and not simply repeating or reproducing it" (2004, 107). Now that you've finished the book, do you agree or disagree with the premise that it is possible to teach English to change the world? Why do you feel this way? How do your views shape your teaching?